CINDERELLA AND HER SISTERS

The Envied and the Envying

by Ann and Barry Ulanov

Cinderella and Her Sisters

The Envied and the Envying

by
Ann and Barry Ulanov

DAIMON

This book is a reworked and expanded version of the book,
Cinderella and Her Sisters, published in 1983
by The Westminster Press, Philadelphia.

Second Printing 2000

Cover picture: 19th century steel engraving

Library of Congress Cataloging in Publishing Data

Ulanov, Ann Belford and Barry.
  Cinderella and Her Sisters.

  Includes index.
  1. Envy. I. Ulanov, Barry. II. Title.

ISBN 3-85630-563-7

Printed in Canada

For our sisters,
Alix and Judith,
who are in no way like Cinderella's

Contents

Preface

a betrayal y
the good in us

Envy is an emotion we all know about, scholars, psychoan-
alysts, and theologians included, but we rarely talk about it,
and very little is written about it. The reason for this silence is
the painful, searing effects of envy. It burns into us like acid,
whether we are the envied or the envying.

But envy really does exist and work its destruction, all the
more successfully because we refuse to face it. In essence,
envy is an attack on being – the being of the envied and of the
envier, too – and an attack on the good quality or stuff that is
envied. Unimpeded, envy would eviscerate everyone and
everything, leaving nothing but shells. Then, perhaps, its own
envious clamoring could rest, but only as long as nothing
appeared to activate its venom anew.

If we refuse to talk about our experiences of envy we
conspire with its savage attempts to annihilate the good,
anything that is in any way good, however we define it. For
finally, envy between persons is a displacement of our own
relation to the good. When Cinderella's sisters envy her, they
get off the hook of their struggle with themselves and their
relation to the good. They dodge trying to relate to their own
selves by means of noisy accusations directed against Cinderella. They avoid figuring out their relation – to their mother,
to the prince, or to what they see as the good life. Instead of
inspecting and muddling along in these real relationships,
they mount vociferous attacks on Cinderella. All the sisters'
energies go into trying to destroy Cinderella's being instead of
trying to take hold of their own, sexually and spiritually.

If we can suffer consciously the envy we ourselves feel,
whether coming from us or at us, it can be a means of
recovering being for us. Envy can lead us to what needs repair

in our identities, in our sexuality and our spiritual centers, and in our efforts to relate to the good. And envy can point us toward the very good that undergirds both the pain and the healing. Envy, so spoiling and injurious, can, if suffered consciously, point us toward the good we thirst for. Envy, that great distance maker, that connection destroyer, can, if suffered consciously, close the gap that its own wounding operations have opened.

We wrote this book to open up this wounded space in human relationships. The Cinderella tale, so simple and so profound, offers a direct road into and through the thickets of envying and being envied. Envy between sisters, between mothers and daughters, between the sexes, between nations; inwardly, between different parts of our own psyche; envy even of God – these are the multiple places of wounding we touch in this book. The central role of envy in determining the very nature of our society – its politics, for example – is, we think, crucial.

The first part of the book explores envy psychologically, what it feels like to be envied and to envy (Chapters 1 and 2); the archetypal background of envy found in relation to the mother (Chapter 3); envy between the sexes (Chapter 4), and the envy that attacks the good itself, the very thing that envy longs for (Chapter 5). We use the Cinderella tale to approach and address these tortuous emotions, taking her and her sisters as two sides of the same envy complex that exists in most of us. Recognizing that in each of us are both sides of the envy drama leads to specific steps to treat the problem (Chapter 6).

The second part of the book explores envy theologically, recognizing that envy has been seen as a major sin through the ages (Chapter 7). It affects our spiritual integrity (Chapter 8) and has specific consequences for our sexual identity, too (Chapter 9). Through Cinderella, whom we see as a kind of female Christ figure, we catch a glimpse of the plight of the good – in theological terms, of God – when in our envy we refuse it and take offense at it (Chapter 10). What solace, then, offers itself to those who suffer the scourge of envy? The answer is in the good itself, which moves us to look at it through the very envy that would attack it (Chapter 11), to go with its little bits and pieces, willingly trying to fit them together into a larger whole of self and community (Chapters 12 and 13). We conclude with a look at the amazing nature of goodness that may gradually become evident in the envy experience, its abundance, its ability to link and make wholes of disparate parts, its abiding presence, and its joy (Chapter 14).

A glossary of terms and a brief review of the psychological literature on envy conclude the book.

We would like warmly to acknowledge the irreplaceable skill and helpfulness of Staley Hitchcock in typing the manuscript.

Ann and Barry Ulanov
Woodbury, Connecticut

Part One

Psychological Explorations

Introduction

The story of Cinderella and her sisters endures as no other fairy tale does. For most of us it is alive in Charles Perrault's late seventeenth-century version, complete with stepmother, fairy godmother, mice, pumpkin, glass slipper, and rescuing prince. For others, there are tellings that reach back in time as much as a thousand years and across the world from the Indians of North America to the peoples of Africa and China. The variations are many, the emphases different, the central figure sometimes not so pure as Cinderella in the more than seven hundred attempts to tell this tale.

Why should this story attract so many tellers, capture so many readers and listeners? What is there about it that cuts through major differences of time, place, and culture? There are other attractive heroines. There are other cruel stepmothers and ugly sisters to bring alive the perils of family life. Rescuing princes abound and if other godmothers, or ingenious animals, or talking fish, or enchanted forests are not necessarily so resourceful as Cinderella's, enough magic exists in the world of fairy tales to provide contentment to an audience hungry for happy endings magically contrived.

None of these things accounts for the hold of Cinderella upon our imagination. Rather, there is something primordial about Cinderella and her tale. Seated in her nest of ashes, she speaks to us of misery in archetypal terms. She is, with whatever degree of natural or supernatural significance we may want to endow her, the Suffering Servant. What is more, she not only serves hard and cruel masters – or more precisely, mistresses – but does so as one called to better things, by inner and outer nobility, by blood, and by spirit. She is, in fact, so much the very essence of the noble that we can accept the fact that she is an enviable creature, and is envied, by her stepmother and sisters, even in her condition, down with the grease and dirt, doomed to endless service and suffering.

The story of Cinderella is the story of envy. It is the epochal tale, even in its usual few pages, of this much-felt, much-endured, but scarcely discussed human emotion. Accounted by tradition second only to pride of the so-called seven deadly sins, envy remains on the outskirts of religious, philosophical, literary, and psychological discourse. It has its place in moral theology and philosophical ethics, but not one commensurate with the stern and nasty language used to describe it and to cast it from the precincts of proper behavior. It has a significant book unto itself in sociology and a few articles in anthropological journals. It gets occasional attention from political scientists, but rarely is any attempt made to understand or explain its pivotal role in motivating events as large as revolution or as shattering as family violence. It has its brief innings in Dante, in John Bunyan, in medieval and Renaissance epic, in some few modern novels, but it lives, even in its most brilliant evocations, only for a moment, personified in such ugly trappings that it is easy to dismiss from consciousness.

Where envy survives – and oh, how it does! – is in human affairs, in little ones and big ones, in major and minor events, but most importantly in the ordinary daily lives of ordinary people, in all of us, one way or another, as enviers or envied. However badly or well we enact the roles, we are called upon at some time or other to play Cinderella or her stepmother or stepsisters.

Freud's deliberations on penis envy have made that phrase a commonplace in our time, and the matching compliment paid the other sex in later psychological theory with envy of breast or vagina has begun to make its way into something like universal conversation. But neither kind of yearning for missing sexual anatomy or function has quite established envy at the center of thought or investigation in depth psychology, though Melanie Klein did find in envy a clue to major truths about human behavior, and did see envy as a constant factor in our lives.

Klein's investigations and all the work done on envy begin from the point of view of the envier.[1] We propose to start from the experience of being envied. This departure brings new light to the complexity of envy – both its miseries and its hidden values – and illuminates more of the archetypal background shared by the envied and the envier.

What happens to one who is being looked at enviously, with the fierce scrutiny and malicious intent that the root meaning for envy – *invidere* or *invidia* – conveys? How does envy appear to Cinderella, the envied one, the object of her sisters' eviscerating examination? What does being envied tell us about the dynamics and effects of envy? What archetypal issues relating to the good confront us here? How can we respond to envy, whether it comes at us or from us? What insight does psychotherapy give us to help us to deal with envy?

Cinderella and her sisters show us the energies of envy – its vicious attack, its determination to spoil all it confronts, its refusal of the good at the same time that, in secret, it spies on the good. The emphasis in Cinderella and her sisters is on envy between women, but the archetypal themes of the tale serve as a means to interpret envy in men as well, envy toward women and toward the feminine elements of their own being. In addition, Cinderella and her sisters represent central aspects of the female personality, and especially the conflict between ego and shadow.

Our interpretation of the tale, therefore, will move back and forth between internal issues: how our own feminine and masculine parts fit or do not fit together, and external issues: how we conduct our life with persons of the same and opposite sexes, how we conflict, compete, or join harmoniously with others. First and foremost, however, we must enter into the awful places where envying and being envied rule. For there, where all of us are bound to spend some of our lives, we will find the reasons why envy is so little dealt with and why it is essential to face it.

1

Being Envied

To be the object of envy is a terrible experience. We know that from our earliest reading. Whether it comes in the form of the scheming plots of Snow White's stepmother to kill the beautiful child, or the sadistic demands of Cindèrella's sisters, designed to humiliate her, or the determination of the two sisters in the fairy tale "One-Eye" to take all the food for themselves and leave their long-suffering sister to starve, envy makes the misery of others its devoted aim.

One who is envied feels the attack of envy as nullification of her own subjective reality. She is turned into an object by her envier, whether by praise or scorn. Her reality as a person is obliterated. Her hurt, her anger, or her shock in response to envious assault seems not to matter at all to the envier. Any facts of her personal history are utterly discounted. That Cinderella, for example, is also the much-loved daughter of a shared father, or that she has suffered the loss of her beloved mother, arouses no sympathy in the envious sisters. Or, to take an example from analytic practice, when a woman, envied by her sister, protests that she too has problems to overcome and that she has worked hard to achieve the good position that is now the target of her sibling's envy, she is met only by the stony face of her envious sister.[2] These facts in her own history make no dent in her sister's envy; they are simply not taken in. The envied one no longer exists as a valid subject.

She is changed into a thing, a mere object of envy. She exists only with reference to the envier's idealization and persecution, typical defenses against the pain that comes with envying.

In idealization, the envier inflates the envied into one "too good to be true," one so far beyond the envier, and in fact all human proportions, that the envier need not feel maliciously competitive. The envied one is turned into a demigod and coerced into accepting that role. In persecution, the same defense mechanism operates, only at the opposite end of the scale. Now the envied one is seen as completely bad and as aiming above all else to make the envier's life miserable. The envier then need not deal with her own envying because it is projected onto the envied one, who can then be blamed for it. The cause of envy lies not in oneself but in the envied one; accusation substitutes for self-examination. In both idealization and persecution, the envied one is turned into an abstraction – hero or villain – and robbed of concrete identity.

Envy generalizes. It blanks out persons in favor of qualities, and even those are not the particular qualities possessed by individual persons but part of a generalized ideal denied the envier by the mere fact of possession by the envied. Here begins that terrible mixture of pain and pleasure which envy always brings with it. The envier may take some pleasure in accounting, finally, for the misery felt in his or her lack of something. But there is great pain, too, not only the original anguish, but a new one. For the immediate effect of turning someone else into an abstraction is to do the same to oneself. One has moved from one's own special case into the great gulf of generalization, where there are no persons but only great frightening qualities.

From the side of the envied one, to be envied is a threatening experience. One feels canceled, no longer validated by reference to one's own particular identity, one's own motives or feelings. All that matters now is the perception of the envier who sees the envied one only in terms of the role he or she plays in the envier's personality. The envying sister in the case example above complained that if her sister did not always look so nice and do so well, then she would feel better about her own self and not feel so inferior. In the face of this attitude the envied one feels cut off at her roots, severed from personal connection to the resources of her own being. Her being fully alive and growing is taken as an intentional doing against her sister. She feels negated in herself and co-opted into another's scheme of things. She is a country invaded and annexed by an enemy, seen now only in terms of service to this hostile neighbor who appropriates both one's past and future by invalidating one's autonomous existence in the present. The envied one really cares about relationship to the envier and is trying somehow to reclaim it, but she inevitably must fail. The envied one feels trapped behind thick glass where she can see the other person and be seen but what she says cannot reach through the thick wall of projection the envier has thrown up against her. In this setting, we all become things, mere objects.

In personal terms, the envied experiences transmutation from subject into object as being utterly cast adrift. It is as if one has become a garbage can into which all the tainted stuff of the envier can be dumped. The envied one is reduced to the envier's projections. Human relationship with the envier is blocked, any bond of sympathy or understanding severed.

This accounts for the second outstanding mark of being envied: utter helplessness. The envied one feels that the connection with the envier has been broken, hacked off as one might destroy a rope bridge. This leaves the envied one impotent, for the connection has been broken off from the other side and there is no way to mend it from this side. The envied one soon learns that any efforts to be nice will only intensify the break. Angry confrontations are taken as justification for grudges. Efforts to understand are labeled as patronizing. Showing the pain caused by the envious attack is met by an ungiving hostile silence. The envied one is clearly being perceived through a distorting lens, so any reparative gestures must appear lopsided and wrong. The envied one is left dependent on the envier to fix the break, something the envier clearly does not want to do. Cinderella's sisters scorn all her efforts to reach them.

The envied one comes smack up against the limits of his or her power to do anything to mend the break or reopen the relationship. The envied has run into a wall with no opening and no way around it. He or she must just accept the wall, and stop trying to get over it. The envied one is powerless against the assault of envy. Such helplessness may cure the envied one of all remaining shreds of omnipotence, but it also will undermine any realistic sense of power to do something or to be someone of consequence.

To be envied is to be attacked. That is the third mark of the experience. Not only is one violated by being made into an object, cut off, and helpless; one is also actively persecuted. The response is anger and fear. One feels under threat of being robbed, not only of specific advantages or attributes one may possess, but in some uncanny way of one's very substance. To the envied one, the envy defies causality, and takes on a tinge of madness. After all, what did one do to provoke this awful malevolence? One did nothing against the envier, did not try to thwart, oppress, or malign the other. Often, in fact, the envied one is a source of help, friendly interest, or active support to the envying. Cinderella cooks, cleans, and sews for her sisters. All the more astounding then is their sudden burst of active malice.

Helmut Schoeck, in his sociological study of envy, makes the same point about the envy shown by undeveloped countries to those countries which have acted as their benefactors. Generosity has aroused ingratitude and hateful resentment, because the lavish giving seems to demonstrate the giver's superiority. Logic fueled by envy can reach so far as to reason that something must be basically wrong or unfair about Western society because life is so good there. Rather than receive, envy wants to destroy the giver, pushing for a leveling down so all will be equally miserable. Schoeck quotes

Nietzsche: "If I cannot have *something*, no one is to have *anything*, no one is to *be* anything."[3]

If the envied can avoid being overwhelmed by defensive expostulation: "What did I ever do to you?" "Haven't we been your great supporters?" or by urges to persecute the envier in retaliation, an extraordinary fact will emerge: the very existence of the envied is the problem. The target of envy's attack is not one's doing, but one's *being*. Cinderella, for example, owns nothing but her work and the attitude with which she approaches it. But her sisters envy her even that. Owning much but doing nothing, they envy her way of being and going about things. They aim to take it out of her, to disembowel her spiritually, so to speak. Seated in her ashes, going cheerfully about her duties, dressed in rags, the suffering servant has an unmistakable allure about her that the envious sisters clearly lack. Somehow they must remove it – which is to say, must remove her. This life-attacking attitude of envy shows most painfully when a parent envies a child, seeing in the child's eager young existence something the parent lacks. It may be a particular talent, physical beauty, or simply the child's youth, its new life.

The envied one often feels stunned at this revelation that his or her being is the problem to the envier, and feels even more helpless to do anything as a result. For what is there to do? Like a victim of racial or sexual prejudice, the envied feels an essential self is under attack, not some fault or virtue that is changeable or detachable from one's central identity. Instead, one's very hold on life, one's connection to the good, is the problem.[4] As a result, hurting envious action is experienced as all the more senseless and without cause. Worse, the envier's touch of venom toward the envied reveals a hostility to good itself.

The envier wants to damage, to degrade, and, in Klein's now famous words, to spoil the goodness of the envied one. Cinderella is exactly as sisters and stepmother want to see her, dirty from the muck of her chores, shabby in rags, deprived, and clearly not worthy to go to the ball. They want to push onto Cinderella their own disfiguring envy – one version of the tale is called "Scar face" – projecting onto her their life-spoiling envy. Thus, they put Cinderella in the death place, among the ashes.

The spiteful effects of envy appear everywhere. Political efforts to destroy benefactor countries result in a hollow triumph for envy. No one gets anything; everyone feels attacked and cheated. Parents who envy their child know the specific torment envy brings: it maims the thing they love. The robbery of being is the ultimate effect. The envying try wildly to gather being up and run off with it, a person's, a group's, a nation's. Failing to do so, they will attack it, vandalize it, so that it is wrecked and of no use anymore to any one, least of all, they hope, to the envied.

The person who is looked at with envy's intensity must beware, for temptations lie on all sides. The blast of envy brings many aftershocks, any one of which can knock over the envied. Pain comes as the first shock. Envy wounds. The envied one falls into the pool of victimization, thrashing around in undeserved hurt. One may struggle to master the pain by self-accusation, making oneself the cause, taking responsibility for the other's projections, denying the malevolence of the envying. Such omnipotence simply compounds the envier's attack with self-attack. The envied may also yield to the opposite temptation, retaliating and persecuting in kind, hoping to expose to everyone how cold, unethical, and grasping the envier is. But this way the envied becomes the backbiter and malicious gossiper.

When the persecution infects the envied, an all-consuming rage against the envier turns in on the envied one, producing an equally thorough guilt. One woman said she felt guilty for being alive because her very existence provoked such unhappy envy in her sister. She wanted to cut herself down so that her sister could thrive. Indeed, she gave up certain activities that her sister found appealing, simply to leave the field open to her sibling. Either way, rage-filled persecution of the envier or of oneself only makes things worse. The poison of envy fills the soul of the envied one.

Withdrawal offers another temptation to the envied. One wants to hide and not tangle with such viciousness, somehow to secure a place safe from contamination. This quitting of the field often excites more attack from the envier, who wants both to preserve this confounding source of the pleasures and pains of envy and to wipe it out. Thus the envier moves in, either for the kill or with a compulsive frenzy to get some kind of more telling response from the envied one, violent if necessary. The envier cannot tolerate simple withdrawal. It feels to the envier as if the envied one were absconding with the good. It must be pursued, or at least dented. One woman caught in an envious situation at work tried to retire from the battle, only to find ugly signs posted on her office door.

An odd but not infrequent variation on the temptation to withdrawal is the envied one's attempt to become entirely self-sufficient, to deny normal dependencies and needs for relationship, especially to potential enviers. The devilish thing about envy, however, is that most often it springs up in close relationships in one's family or working life, from which one cannot withdraw. How then to deny reliance upon the other, whether co-worker, neighbor, sibling, or parent? The envied one seeks refuge from envy by no longer looking to the envier for anything, trying to become both provider and dependent, lover and beloved, teacher and learner, even, if necessary, male and female. This can sometimes result in a remarkable development of talent and splendid independence, but it will not last. Eventually, chronic loneliness, even schizoid isolation, will develop. The withdrawal will have ended where it started, in a diminishing of being.

But all this maneuvering to avoid envy only attracts more of it. The envied one who is successful in denying dependence on others makes the self into the enviable object *par excellence.* The envied one shows nothing that would contradict the idealization the envier projects, and thus arouses even more excited envy. To the envier, the idealized one seems to be intentionally hoarding the good and withholding it.[5]

The envied grow increasingly desperate, for nothing succeeds in warding off envy. If they renounce any hope of being seen and accepted as themselves, they are accused of being cold and aloof. If they try to share their good, they are attacked for showing off or being patronizing.[6] If they try to defend by explaining, they are not listened to, for explanations will not fill up an empty envier. Even if some of the melodrama is lacking, they are in the position of hostages being held by terrorists. There is nothing they can do to appease their captors. Least of all do the enviers want to lose hold of the envied, to let the hostages get away.

Withdrawal from envy, whether from the envier or into oneself, meets a dead end, and frequently catapults the envied one into the opposite temptation: to try to do something to fix the break and reestablish contact. Simone Weil reminds us of how much evil is set in motion by hasty interfering actions.[7] These efforts usually prove futile because in them the envied one begins from a wrong premise. Nothing the envied one can do will repair the break because it came from the envier's side. Often efforts to help the envier are only attempts to ward off this blow to one's omnipotence. In analysis, for example, an analyst can overinterpret on such occasions, trying to appease a patient's envy by explanation. But such explaining (especially if correct!) pulls both analyst and analysand above the level of conflict, when what is needed is to get grounding in the envious emotion that exists between them. These efforts collapse quickly. The patient spits out all the forced food and the analyst gets fed up. What is more, the envier usually retaliates against such intrusive goodwill with an even more savage attack.

Goodness figures centrally in the last great temptation for the envied one: to deflect the attack of envy by altogether disowning the good that is the target of the attack. "That is not mine," one says at such a point; "I don't know about that; it doesn't belong to me." The envied one is saying, in effect: "I am no different from you. I do not have anything you would want. Why, I am really no better than you!" This refusal to own the good that belongs to one, indeed what one may have worked long and hard to reach, is a serious blow aimed at goodness, even at being itself. The result is more trouble for both envier and envied.

The envied one's denial of the envied good threatens to remove all goodness from the scene. Jesus warns us about the fate of those who deny him: they too shall be denied. Those who will not use the talents given them will lose them altogether and be delivered into outer darkness. The snarling tangle that ensues between the envier and the envied is an all-too-graphic example of what that darkness can be like. The envier experiences the other's denial of goodness as a deliberate hiding of the good in order not to share it.[8] The envier's frenzy of persecutory reaction reaches fever pitch. The envied one, in turn, suffers the misery of cowardice, knowing the pain of conscious shrinking from the truth, throwing it away in order to play safe. The envied one now feels a deep dread of the good, falling into the temptation to hold goodness itself responsible for the envious attack that has brought so much pain. How long can one feel pleased with something that brings such opprobrium on oneself? Wouldn't it be better to be less talented, less virtuous, less subject to envy? If the good could just be abandoned, then one would be secure. Better to turn away from the good, pretend it is not good after all, or does not even exist.

2

Envying

The envier also dreads the good in a deep way, and much of
the spoiling activity of envy operates to cope with this dread.
Above all, the envier feels empty of the good and hungers after
it ferociously. A woman patient describes this experience in
frantic terms, saying: "I'm starving! I'm suffocating!" She is
conveying her panic that she could not get enough of the good
to survive. This hunger and accompanying panic account for
the confusion of envy with greed. Though we often experience
the two together, they differ in precise ways, as Melanie Klein
shows. Greed operates primarily by the process of introjection: taking in the outer object, positively swallowing it whole,
exhausting it of its goodness, even destroying it in the urgency
to gobble up all its substance for oneself. In greed, we do not
concern ourselves with the fate of the object; often we still try
to take substance from it long past its willingness or ability to
give. Mothers, for example, may feel "eaten alive" by their
infants. But in greed our intent is to stuff ourselves, not to hurt
the object. Any damage done is a mere by-product.[9]

. In contrast, envy aims to hurt and spoil the object, to empty
it of its good stuff, whether or not we can acquire it. Envy, in
this sense, is more social than greed. But it sees only part of
an object, never the whole. It fastens on the desired part and
reduces the object to that part. Instead of taking in anything,
envy operates by projection, thrusting its own spoiling, spite-

ful, destructive feeling of envy onto an object. Cinderella's sisters, for example, must force her into a degraded condition, reducing her to ashes, to discarded rags and refuse. Thus, by projection, they acquire a fitting vehicle for their own sense of living on mere scraps of life, feeling as they do that no one ever gives anything to them, that others always get more. Others are to blame, then, and must pay for it.

Classical descriptions of envy paint an equally ugly picture. Spenser portrays envy riding on a "ravenous wolf.... Between his cankered teeth a venomous toad." The poison runs all over his face, "For death it was, when any good he saw," and we can conclude that he sees much, for his coat is painted "full of eyes." The classical personification of envy is as a hater of others' joy or prosperity or, worst of all, confidence in religion or any truth that can be found in words. The mere holding of principles of faith is enough to gain Envy's attack in Bunyan's *The Pilgrim's Progress.* Marlowe's Envy says, "I cannot read, and therefore wish all books were burnt." The details are few in these and other literary testimonies of the same kind, but the point is almost always the same: envy attacks, envy denies, envy eviscerates.[10]

Right on the heels of the hungry emptiness of envy, or mixed in with it, is the envier's experience of being persecuted by the good. The good threatens to overwhelm the envier's fragile and nascent sense of self. It is felt as "too much to bear," as "more than I can stand," to quote the words of several patients.

One woman described the goodness she dreaded as "a huge inflatable balloon that you somehow swallowed. Then it would expand and take up all the room, filling up every space inside you, squeezing you out." The good intrudes and occupies rather than feeds. Another patient spoke of "being flooded" with goodness that simply set her adrift. Still another woman saw goodness as an invader she met in a terrifying nightmare. In it, "a big, blunt-nosed, plump, rounded fish beaches itself near me and some other females. One of them, a naked girl, tries to help the fish. She puts her arm around it to stroke it. But the fish clamps its mouth shut on her hand and dives swiftly into the water, pulling the girl in after it, and then rushes to the deepest place it can find. The woman cannot get her hand free without pulling it off. She fears she will drown. She is screaming under water!"

The dreamer associated to this horrifying image her experience of her mother when she was a little girl. Her mother would give lavishly, energetically, and generously of special foods, outings, shopping trips, presents of all kinds. But rather than feeling endowed by these gifts, the daughter felt seized, dragged under, covered up by her mother's goodness. She could not take it in because it utterly effaced her, leaving her no room to breathe, drowning her. But refusing her mother's goodness left her hungry and in danger of starvation. Her rejection so angered her mother she would turn away from her altogether. The daughter felt crazy and guilty as a result. Her mother was giving and giving, yet she did not feel being given to. She wanted so much to receive but could not take in anything. She wanted to connect with her mother, but all she did was to reject her and to feel rejected by her.

Her mother's goodness felt to her like the menacing dream fish – an odd male-female fish, shaped like a breast and a penis, something darting up at her from another dimension. It elicited a sympathetic response, but "once you touched it, especially if you were young and naked of any defenses, it clamped down on you and dragged you off to its lair." It was alive to the dreamer as both an intrusive sexual organ and an undersea monster of great psychological intensity.

The fish is like a phallic part of the female self – what Jung calls the animus – not yet differentiated into a distinct part or integrated into female identity. It shows great power and thrust, but its power is at odds with the standpoint of the dreamer and of the women on the shore. In this form the fish's power is menacing and, rather than connecting the dreamer's ego to the deeps, threatens to drown it. As the dreamer's associations made clear, the fish's power was like her mother's goodness, a goodness mixed up with terrifying aggression.

The Jungian Erich Neumann talks about this image of the mother as the phallic mother, a still undifferentiated, male-and-female mother.[11] Harold Searles talks from a neo-Freudian perspective about a mother who contributes to the schizophrenic disorder of her child as a woman whose aggression is not yet separated from her loving, with the result that her primitive form of love is felt by her and her child to be dangerous.[12]

The dreamer's mother and the dreamer's own psyche were in this kind of undifferentiated state. Like her mother, she felt sudden impulses to give or to be given to, impulses not harmonized with the rest of her personality. Both dragged her under, so to speak, rather than connecting her to satisfying experiences as giver or receiver.

That the fish grabbed the girl's hand points to the specific place of missed childhood connection between mother and daughter, and later between ego and self, symbolized in the dream as girl and fish. That the personal connection is missing is represented in the dream by the threat of the girl's hand being torn off. In fact, the good things her mother gave her were not given personally to *her*, hand to hand, so to speak. She experienced her mother's giving as "a relief to *her* [the mother], not specifically something for me. I would be eaten if I let her feed me." What was missing was what D. W. Winnicott calls an appropriate object presentation, timed to a specific child by a sensitive mother.[13] What the mother gave was irrelevant. It did not focus on her daughter's immediate need. The giving was crude, general, invading, however generous. The child was a "subjective object" to her mother, seen not as a distinct, autonomous self, but only there as something to be used, to play a part in the mother's need for self-expression. Just like the envied one, the child is thus turned into an object. In this sense a child is a part-object idolized by the mother for the role it plays in the mother's personality. In Jung's terms, the ego-self axis is faulty, swamped from the self's side. The young ego is flooded by an uncaring self without reference to the concrete needs and limits of the ego. The self assimilates it rather than feeds it.[14]

Such experience can produce an abysmal confusion, as in this dreamer's case. For self-preservation can be obtained only by refusal of the good stuff needed to survive. One must alienate the very source on which one feels dependent. The result? One feels "bad," "ungrateful," "hard to please," "guilty." Above all, one feels dread of the good that one so desires. For in the presence of such a suffocating goodness, one feels starved not fed, persecuted not nourished, under threat of annihilation instead of supported in one's being.

In severe instances, this sort of confusion can engender psychotic episodes. The parent may envy the child, which makes the parent treat the child like a part of the parent, and never really give anything to the child at all. The child may envy the parent simply because the parent has the stuff to give and therefore the good remains outside the child's control. Each leads to the same impasse: the parent cannot enjoy the good the child brings and the child cannot take in the good the parent offers. In the midst of so much food, each goes hungry. Both feel bad about the good and repudiate it, or they feel good about the bad because it does not threaten them the way the good does. Good and bad get all mixed up. For the child, especially, no good is lodged securely enough so that the young ego can identify with it and grow strong. The child is left then with fragments that conflict and compete but do not fit together. The puzzle is all parts that do not make up a whole.[15]

Even more confusing is the fact that the envy which causes this confusion about goodness may also be grabbed at as a means to dissipate it. Envy seems to offer a way to handle this desperate suffering: One envies the good in the other. One wants to spoil it, because it originates outside oneself and remains outside one's control. But envying keeps the much-desired good in sight. So out of envy one tries to steal the good as the only possible way to possess it and yet keep it at a safe distance. One persecutes the good because one cannot take it in, but this way one nevertheless goes on being involved with it. The different levels and the different routes of envy make this clear.

At a basic level, envying allows one to admit a voracious hunger for the good, but it is a hunger experienced as emptiness, through frustration rather than satisfaction. Repeated experiences of being overwhelmed by feedings that cancel one's subjective existence (either by too much or too little food) leave an envier unable to eat. There are mothers who are overeager – what Harry Guntrip calls the "doing breast" – who cannot wait for their babies to signal readiness to eat.[16] They insist greedily on their own pace. Such a mother's milk floods her infant's emerging appetite. This kind of giving is in fact a firm denial.

An analyst, too, can flood a patient with interpretations in response to persistent cries for help and demands to know what to do. But a patient, like an infant, must reject the food thus evoked as "too much," or as inappropriate, in that often repeated remark that what the analyst says may be "intellectually right, but not where I live." One woman in analysis complained of forgetting everything said in the sessions, presenting herself at each subsequent session in the original empty state. It took a while to realize that that was the point: to experience the emptiness first, and only then, afterward, to inquire how to fill it.

On a second level of envy, stealing the good seems the only way to relate to it because open acknowledgment would end up forcing one to rob oneself. One patient confessed she resisted getting well for fear it would put a feather in the analyst's professional cap. She dreamed she had baked a wonderful pie, her particular cooking specialty, and that then the analyst took credit for it. She rejected anything said in the session but eventually confessed she would feed on it between sessions. This was like eating in secret, getting fed without having to admit dependence on the feeder. Sharing the good came only at a later point.

The stealing activity merges with the third level of envy which directs persecution and hateful attack on the good that one sees in another, and even on goodness itself. At this level, the hungry emptiness is so acute, and what one can steal seems so little, that the envier feels greatly endangered. The only way to manage such deprivation is to turn it into active hating of what one desires. The good itself becomes the enemy.

In personal relations, the envier projects onto the envied one the excellence that seems so out of reach, or fastens on some skill or wit already in the envied one's personality. Either way, the envier manages relation to the good by seeing it as existing only somewhere else, in others, never in oneself. The envier goes further, and attributes to the envied an active intent to hoard the good, tantalizing even more the envier's raging hunger.

The envier now can make sense of the deeply felt inner emptiness and muddling confusion and distance from the good. It is the envied one's fault, intentionally depriving the envier! Cinderella's sisters blame her for their wretchedness. Burning hate and attack are now the only means of relating to the good. Those people who possess it must be punished! Finally, at this degree of envying we accuse the good itself of retreating from our reach, deliberately evading us. Under such distress we even reproach God.

Dealing with this sort of destructive attitude in analysis makes for explosive moments. The first encounter with this sort of furious, envying transference makes an analyst tremble. Something like hatred radiates from the analysand, and can erupt in vindictive repudiation of any effort to narrow the gulf between patient and therapist. What has to be learned is that the rage is in fact a kind of connection, one to be experienced and not too quickly resolved. The good projected onto the analyst is often so idealized and so far removed from reality that the only way the envier has of connecting to it is by attack. The envier in these moments knows a Luciferian despair of ever being able to receive from or give to the good.

That is when the envier is tempted to disavow the good altogether and indulge in an orgy of wrecking. At best, the envier scores a pyrrhic victory, leaving him feeling burned-out and in despair.

The analyst must move carefully here, choosing between experiencing a patient's attacks and not putting up with them, for the patient is really terrified that his spoiling tactics will succeed and will ruin the relationship to the analyst. At periodic points an analyst must just stop the wrecking and guard the analytic connection from the perils of "acting out."[17] The patient is testing to see whether the relationship is strong enough to withstand the hating envy. Security is gained only when reliable limits are set, those strong enough to be banged against and still survived.

The place envy occupies in our psyches and its effects on our development show three possible routes. At its worst, envying uses up a lot of psychic energy and interrupts development in major ways. It produces a state of confusion between good and bad objects. Attacking the good, as we have seen, replaces actually taking it in, and leaves our inner world devoid of the nurturing objects with which the nascent ego can identify and form its own strong core. Like Lucifer, we resent the fact that we are ourselves not the origin of good, that we do not control and own it, and we angrily refuse it, quitting the scene to set up a realm where we can rule instead.

When this envying occurs at a very young age, a child's ego never adequately consolidates or masters the processes of give-and-take with the warmth or support carried by others, or the liveliness and comfort offered to the child in images from its own unconscious. Instead, envying undercuts the whole process and diverts energy into complicated and wasteful defenses in which the good is seen as bad and the bad as good. These defenses often proceed to manufacture a narcissistic character disorder, a schizoid condition, or even a full-sized paranoia that may reach psychotic proportions.[18] The major blow to the psyche falls on the ego, which cannot form a core of identity securely in touch with others and open to spontaneous images from the unconscious. Instead, the ego must guard itself and surreptitiously scheme to get what it thinks it needs to survive. It is poor in identity, as terrible a poverty as we can face.

Melanie Klein describes the sad fate of such an impoverished ego which, failing to take in the good must attack it instead. Envying is then taken up by the superego, which grows unduly harsh and assails the individual's assertive and creative capacities in retaliation. If we try to make a good object into an ideal, all-perfect one, we feel even more abandoned. We see it as too good to be true; it seems to be mocking us from its superior height, like king to peasant. As the gap widens, envy grows and sets out to dethrone the good.

Envy interferes with any effort to make amends or restitution, lest one really does repair the object and lose one's superiority to it. One ends up feeling guilty, and worse, hopeless, about a way out. For if the good object is acknowledged as good or restored to its undamaged state, then its very goodness incites a new envying and the vicious cycle starts all over again.[19]

In Jungian language, the vicious cycle is set in motion when the infant ego fails to differentiate from its original self. Ordinarily, the self gives rise to the ego by spontaneously breaking up into parts that form the basis for the archetypal images which underlie the ego's growth into a distinct personality. The ego then can develop over against the self's archetypes and the mother and the world.[20] Envy sabotages this process of ego differentiation and identity formation.

The infant's envy, or the envy of any of us when our egos are fragile, prevents differentiation from the all-in-all self by massive and affective blocking of the precise parts we envy. Instead, the object of envy – in short, the "good" – seems overwhelming to us. We resort then to all the various temptations of the enviers: to feel persecuted by the good and to turn away from it, to want to hurt and spoil it, to fall into confusion of psychotic proportions about the good where we experience the self that could support our egos as annihilating.

The second route that envy can take in our development does not interrupt ego formation but rather impoverishes it. Envy exists strongly, but it is split off from the rest of the personality, which goes on developing more or less normally. The envying emotions, with all their complex interactions, are relegated to an unconscious place, where they operate undifferentiated and confused. In Jungian language, our envy falls into the shadow part of our personality, indeed takes up residence there and threatens our egos. The envious enmity of the sisters toward Cinderella can be read to describe our intrapsychic drama of shadow versus ego. In moments of stress, or as a result of analytic treatment, these envious feelings may come to light, bringing with them intense anxiety, sometimes reaching to psychosis. In this route, envy exists in a pocket of our personality, draining energy from the rest, but not interrupting our growth directly. For example, the guilty feelings (themselves unconscious) aroused by our unconscious envying restrict the pleasure or success or creativity we can allow ourselves. We cannot claim our own identity. If we want to be all of ourselves, or if life forces us to confront all of ourselves, our envying emotions will come to the fore. Then we must work them through. If we do not claim the envy, its presence will unseat the security of all our relations, to ourselves and to others. For envy, always lurking in the background, can at any point break through and poison all interactions.

The sorts of experience that put us under stress and require us to face our hidden pockets of envy can just as well be good experiences as bad. Any attempt at intimacy, for example, really to know and be known by another, to experience parenthood with its demanding intermixings with a child, to use our imagination really to pray – all will bring pressure on our personality, forcing us to acknowledge and to integrate our unconscious envy. On the other hand, efforts to claim, work through, and assimilate our envy can bring great increases of energy – now no longer siphoned off into negative attacks – and a greater capacity to value and to love others because our envy no longer needs to spoil their goodness.[21]

The last route that envy can take is easiest of all, because here envy is modified and even healed by feelings of what Klein calls gratitude. Gratitude includes gratification, a feeling of satisfaction at being in the hands of the good, knowing how pleasing being given to and filled up can be. One takes in the good and feels it living inside as part of one's ego. The good seems close now, not distant and unapproachable. We are emboldened to take in more. Gratification increases and envy decreases, because we experience the good as given to us, as part of us, as really available. Instead of envying it and needing to spoil it, we want to emulate the good. This engenders the use and development of our own assertive creative capacities. We experience the good as quite within our reach. A benevolent linearity replaces the vicious circle of envying and destruction of what we envy.[22] In Jungian language, this last route of envy can be understood as the ego's experience of the self as a constant spur to respond to the self's continued unfolding. The self moves the ego to new experience, and the ego's reception and concretization of new bits of the self ground the interaction between them. In theological language, the ego continues to incarnate the self.

In a startling way, the experiences of the envied and the envier are greatly alike. Both feel invalidated as subjects, turned into someone else's thing, mere objects. Both feel helpless to fix the broken relationship and dependent on the other to repair it. Both feel emptied of goodness. Both feel dread of anything good, which is seen as putting them into a position where their identities can be obliterated. They seem so much the same and yet they are very different beings. The obvious questions are, What do they do? What do we do?

3

Envy of the Mother

Going more deeply into the shared plight of the envied and
the envying brings some light on what to do in the face of
envy. Archetypal pictures are helpful here, precisely because
they are not personal but typological. Cinderella and her
sisters show us types of reactions to envy that we might think
of as surpassing our own gifts and capacities but which
nonetheless can point up the basic issues around goodness
that envy constellates. We need such an archetypal tale, one
that encompasses but also exceeds our personal experience,
precisely because envy has a strong collective life too, as is
evidenced by its common recognition as a universal failing.
That envy is always quickly condemned – and then is just as
quickly put aside – urges us to find ways to understand and
master it. The fairy tale exhibits as few other forms the
archetypal elements of envy upon which we must focus: envy
in relation to the mother, envy between the sexes, envy as a
collective phenomenon in relation to the good. Thus we turn
to Cinderella.

We need fairy tales at the beginning of our conscious lives,
as we need literature later on, to provide us with the essential
metaphors of true and false grace, of sin and virtue, of the
shadowy textures of our lives and all our ways of covering
them up. If Cinderella did not exist, we would have to invent
her.

Investigating the archetypal background of envy points up the central role of the mother. In the Cinderella tale, the mother is the only parent, the father always being "away," absent. No distinct male figure appears in the tale at all until the prince turns up hunting the glass slipper's owner. No male-female couple appears in the tale until the end when Cinderella and the prince meet. The mother figure dominates the story until that time. From the first, she shows a primordial duality of death and life, good and bad, maleness and femaleness.

Cinderella once knew a good mother, now dead, but rediscovered in her fairy godmother. But she also knows a mean stepmother who is quite alive, who envies and persecutes her. Her sisters have their own live mother in this figure. She appears to be good for them, but her effects are in fact all bad. She seems to be advancing their life, but actually brings them only death-in-life, leaving them empty, envious, discontented. This mother figure comprises both mother and father, male and female to her daughters, acting as mock homemaker and nourisher. As promoter of her daughters' life in the world, she tries, but inevitably fails, to engineer their success at the ball. Presumably feeding her daughters, she devours them instead. They exist only as self-objects to her, pawns in her schemes for preferment, power, and prestige. She uses them for her phallic thrusts into the world. She cannot see them as young women in their own right.

By examining the two different responses to the mother that Cinderella and her sisters make, the all-in-all reality of the mother in relation to the origins of envy comes clear. Beginning with the envied Cinderella, we see one half of our response to the good and to being itself that the mother represents. Cinderella knows both a good and a bad mother, and tries hard to deal with each part, wrestling with the inevitable ambivalence of opposites contained in all being. While sitting amid her ashes, she mourns her own dead mother, who was so good and loving to her. The ashes themselves recall the Vestal Virgins tending the hearth of

Hera, the mother goddess, whose fire was never to go out.[23] Ashes also mean purification, as at Ash Wednesday, and stand symbolic of loss and death.

Cinderella's name tells us clearly how she sits there in her ashes – a live, glowing coal, an ember that can at any time burst into flame again. For though she mourns the loss of her good mother as a tangible, outer presence, she does not forget her, she is not separated from her. She longs for such a good source of being again to help and support her. And when such a fabulous creature does appear in the sublimated form of the fairy godmother, Cinderella accepts her gladly.

In many of the tale's versions, a definite link exists between the deceased mother and the magic godmother. Cinderella's real mother leaves her a calf, or a hazel twig, or a date-tree seedling, or a fish, all of which grow to marvelous proportions, with power to feed the girl and endow her with her famous clothing, coaches, and horses to take her to the ball.

Cinderella's loss of her real mother and regaining of a symbolic one can be interpreted as the development of an internal image of goodness taken in from the original mother but refashioned now into its own trustworthy place of inner access to the mother archetype as representative of life's giving and creative depths. She turns the painful loss into an opportunity to approach and make sense of the good whenever and however it may turn up.

Cinderella also knows a bad mother, of course. Her stepmother rejects and reviles her with almost professional skill, actively trying to make her feel inferior and punished. She treats Cinderella with every prejudice, scorn, and scapegoating exclusion. No matter what Cinderella does for her stepmother or sisters, they inevitably shut her out.

In a fairy tale of similar theme, "One-Eye, Two-Eyes, Three-Eyes," her envious sisters persecute Two-Eyes because she has a normal pair of eyes, while they suffer lack or excess. They envy her exactly right proportion. Their disproportion makes her substance hateful. Erich Neumann notes that the scapegoat can sometimes be a superior figure; Cinderella plays that role here, like a female Christ figure, a suffering servant.[24] Jesus as the archetypal scapegoat, brought to death by his enemies' envy, vividly shows the savagery goodness can arouse. The false issue, so tempting to both envier and envied, is to ask, why does one of us have the good and the other not? There can only be one answer: it must be your fault or my fault. Both possibilities are caught in our attempts to control the good and its distribution. Of course, the true issue lies elsewhere, in the problem of how to discover and relate to the good, where to find it, how to nourish it.

What is remarkable about Cinderella is her response to the envy of her stepmother and stepsisters. She does not answer their ugliness; she is not spiteful. She does not in any way identify with the nastiness directed at her, does not treat her family or herself in equally nasty ways. It is not that she is impervious to the envious attacks. She cries. She feels hurt. But she does not wallow in her misery, or blame herself, or run away. She bears with her sisters' ridiculous demands and accepts the tasks given her. She holds on to what her own mother gave her and does not despair. She falls, with the grace that defines her, into the role of suffering servant. She remains true to goodness despite everything that tells against it. And that attitude develops the fullness of her own goodness and deepens our understanding of it with her.

In several versions of the tale, the stepmother says Cinderella can go to the ball only after she has sorted out some good lentils from a mass of spoiled ones which her stepmother has just dumped into the ashes. This task must be repeated three times. Cinderella is helped to do so by a bird that represents the spirit of her dead mother. Here we see dramatized the painstaking work of sifting good from bad, bit by bit, differentiating between them to integrate the one and refuse the other.

The sorting task represents the basic ordering of a woman's ego in relation to her primordial depths, symbolized here by the hearth, which represents the mother archetype. Cinderella chooses between the opposites of being, good and bad, putting them in right relation, picking out what is edible and promotes life from among the dead lentils that must be left to return to their natural state. She needs it all – the incompleteness, the sacrificial role, the energies elicited in her by desertion and betrayal. They prepare her for the machinery of her deliverance. Marie Louise von Franz sees this task as a signal example of female heroism, comparable to a hero's slaying of a dragon and freeing of a people from terror.[25] Cinderella brings a strong, firm consciousness into her hidden background nature, thus setting in order the opposites in her unconscious. What she is doing is constructing an ego-self relation. She does not deny the bad – the spoiled lentils and the ashes; they are there all right. But she does find and secure the good. What the stepmother intended as a degrading task, Cinderella invests with moral stature.

Cinderella thus displays one part of our response to the good and to the origin of being that the mother represents. Cinderella recognizes the gap between herself and the mother figure, a gap symbolized by the death of her own mother on the one hand, and on the other, the inexplicable withdrawal of the good from her, represented by her stepmother's refusal to give her anything. Cinderella feels the hurt of the loss of the good, but holds nonetheless to the little bits of goodness that she has known, despite all her many frustrations and deprivations, whether a cinder among the ashes, like the glowing memory of her mother's love, or a good seed to be rescued from the bad, like her hope to go to the ball despite all signs to the contrary. Cinderella fixes her eye on the good, wherever it is to be found, in however small a portion. She takes what crumbs she can find, but she is also quick to welcome the whole cake when it is offered her. She holds to the good, small or large, and it does not desert her. In theological terms, she is obedient.

In contrast, Cinderella's sisters always fasten on the bad and the way the good is denied them, however little that may be true. Thus they comprise the other half of our response to the good and to the source of being that the mother figure represents. For Cinderella's stepfamily represents a kind of inverted trinity of evil, funny in a macabre or farcical way, deadly in its potentialities. In their mixture of the comically inept and grimly efficient movements of evil, they are like the Charlie Chaplinish grotesque into which Bertolt Brecht made Adolf Hitler.[26]

The stepmother exemplifies that sort of bad parent whose devouring envying schemes to *do* in order to cover up an inability to *be*. She does not feed or love or support her daughters, but consumes their independent selves by using them to plot her own self-advancement. She treats them as her property, as small moons in her destructive orbit, instruments to secure her own status and power.

The stepsisters show all the signs of severe deprivation of the goodness of a mother's love. They whine, they complain, they accuse. Full of "Why didn't you?" and "Why don't you?" and "You're to blame," of "I feel terrible and what are you going to do about it?" they fasten onto Cinderella as the cause and cure for their deprivations, gaining some grim pleasure in trying to make her suffer more than they do. They put their bad feeling onto her. They delight in fording it over her and scorn her efforts to serve them gladly. They see only the bad because they feel so radically empty of the good.

Curiously, it is Cinderella who performs the role of good mother for the sisters. She feeds and cleans them and helps them get ready for the ball, sewing lace and ribbons to make them look pretty. Whatever goodness they see, they see in Cinderella, but they cannot take it in. They see her goodness as only something utterly removed from themselves, to be violated. They cannot take her into full consciousness, for they live in the nothingness of evil. Empty of relation to any good in themselves, they can only envy what they see of it in her, relating to it only negatively by trying to destroy it. Thus the sisters remain hungry, ungrateful, backbiting, insistently and clamorously self-assertive, caught in hostile attitudes to the good, because, fundamentally, they resent its existence as something outside themselves, never under their own control. Their moral attitudes spring from an emptiness that cries out against those who are full. All must be, not just as empty as we, but emptier still, they insist, producing with their cry a destructive energy that can build nothing.

We must take Cinderella and her sisters as showing two opposite human attitudes within each of us to the archetypal mother figure. We are all ambivalent toward her and she shows good and bad faces to all of us. Although theorists of depth psychology differ over whether or not envy exists in us from birth, all recognize it as a common and unavoidable emotion. If considered innate (Melanie Klein, Otto Kernberg, and Jung), envy is said to spring spontaneously from the second of our reactions to the good, as symbolized by the sisters.[27] We do not just admire it and receive it gratefully; we look upon it with hostility because the source of our comfort, food, and love originates outside ourselves. Like the demonic archetype personified as Satan, we turn away from the source precisely because we are not it. Envy extinguishes gratitude. We want to see ourselves as the fountain of goodness. If outer experiences of frustration with our actual mother (or whoever may be the giver of the good at any time for us) combine with inner impulses of envy, so much the worse. For then we impute to the source of goodness an intentional withholding of its riches in order to keep us hungry and miserable. Goodness seems as distant from us, when we are caught by envy of such proportions, as another galaxy.

If we see envy resulting from deprivation (Heinz Kohut, D. W. Winnicott, and Leslie Farber) and arising only after we achieve a rudimentary ego status and concern for the other, envy refers us back to an early and marked disruption of relation to the mother and what she represents.[28] Food, both symbolic and literal, either floods a child, threatening to swamp its tiny ego, or is withheld, not reliably there when needed, or only carelessly given in unpredictable rhythms. The feeding connection can also be disrupted through a bad match between mother and child of physical constitutions and psychic tempos. The child's instinctual potential may be more vigorous than the mother's, truly more than she can handle, or the mother may be coping with illness or tragedy and unable to devote enough attention to her child. The child's instinctual hunger and accompanying fantasies remain unsatisfied and split off from the psyche, thus forming those pockets of unconscious envy and rage that siphon off energy and inhibit growth. If a child gets stuck at this level of anger and frustration, then envy takes the form of a voracious hunger, needing to be concealed even from the child itself, severely repressed to keep its ego from being entirely overwhelmed. Such envy, suffered unconsciously rather than acknowledged, makes one feel an eternal victim, the left-out menial sitting in the ashes, overworked and underappreciated, with a paranoid conviction that others always get more than oneself. This sort of envy, dominated by hunger, centers on the oral stage of development and leads to related disorders – compulsive eating, for example, or its opposite, wild concern about getting fat, either way fearful one could be taken over by this rapacious repressed hunger.[29]

Although envy afflicts both sexes, the fairy tale shows us how particularly poignant it is for women to be victims of maternal envy. For a daughter, a mother embodies the female self in all its symbolic wholeness and integrity. The mother, as the fount of life, displays the great resources of a woman's potential being. If experiences of the mother are associated with massive frustration, a woman's body becomes a closed gate, and her breast a bitter gall. Thus some women's sexual frigidity, or radical difficulty in carrying a pregnancy to term or nursing an infant, can be traced to the influence of unconscious envy. Sometimes a woman can only feel herself to be a self, separate and out of the reach of the negative mother, by denying all her womanly functions. Anything associated with female biological life threatens to suck her back into destructive envious relationship to the mother figure. She feels as distant from her own femininity as she has at other times felt all men to be separated from all things female. She sits in the ashes of a woman's world, another, less graceful Cinderella.

If we feel, either as infants or at any point in our lives where we live even temporarily in dependency on a good outside us, that the good rather than feeding us is starving and abandoning us, we may become so furious that we must project these emotions outward in order to survive them. We put them onto other people and fight them there, which accounts for so many spoiling and hateful assaults on the good. We are consumed with envy of the good because we despair of ever gaining it. The object of our attacks may be the mother or her surrogates, whomever we perceive to hold the good at our expense.

Developmentally, the despoiling behavior occurs at a later stage than the oral, when we have more aggressiveness at our disposal and the ability to direct our venom at a target. All the shadow parts of our personality come into play: the gossip and nasty damning by faint praise, the deliberate refusal of warmth to others, the outright wish to damage someone else's good to avoid seeing that person as superior to ourselves.

An example of envy operating at the Oedipal stage shows when we seek to defeat our rival, not out of love for the third party to whom we both lay claim, but because we begrudge our rival anything we cannot possess. By contrast, in jealousy we aim to possess the beloved and to get rid of the rival. Jealousy is clearly a three-person relationship, where envy concerns only two: the envied and the envier. Jealousy is founded on love for a whole person, where envy reduces the other to a part it wants to ruin if it cannot be appropriated. As Leslie Farber says, the central conflict of envy is a subjective one. Envy is our unhappy response to another's superiority and precludes "rivalry, imitation, or emulation."[30]

Searles gives a grim example of Oedipal envy expressed in the collective sphere as apathy. The older generation is seen as allowing conditions to develop in the world that threaten the existence of the younger generation, such as war or environmental pollution, thus destroying through universal disaster the rival young it failed to vanquish in personal battle.[31]

Envy can be seized upon politically as a force to promote ideology. In former Soviet Russia, for example, children have long been encouraged to inform against their parents, their natural envy being manipulated for the use of the state. Neighbor is used to inform against neighbor, conscripting envy as a weapon of the state. Envy of all who would create something new or develop their own ideas – artist, philosopher, whoever – becomes an article of the party faith. Anyone who deviates from the group identity becomes a target of organized envy and persecution. Thus in former Soviet Russia, as in Nazi Germany, artists are sent to camps or mental asylums for holding "incorrect ideas."[32] As Osip Mandelstam said with wry precision, only in old Russia is poetry taken with such deadly seriousness. He knew. He was imprisoned and executed for a few lightly disparaging lines about Stalin in one of his poems. And we can add, that in such a setting the power of envy is truly recognized. That is why, as Schoeck remarks, left-wing ideologues try to come to power by promising an envy-free society, working to harness the destructive forces of envy for their own purposes. Of course their procedure must lead to disaster, for it ignores the psychic reality of envy, which can never be banished, no more by a government than by a preacher. And envy returns from rhetorical exile with all the vengeance of the repressed. For example, as Schoeck notes, envy disguised as concern for justice always produces an even more tyrannical class than before. In the former USSR of 1960 there was a ratio of maximum to minimum income of 40 to 1 in contrast to a ratio of 10 to 1 in the West.

Trading on envy produces that primitive envy barrier which is so hostile to innovation. Anyone who differs from the group is accused of being against full equality and is invariably punished. The only acceptable situation is one where no one need be envied, for no one possesses the coveted good. Clearly an overstimulated envy must become a dangerous autonomous force of destruction, as Schoeck puts it, "a dynamic which cannot be arrested."[33] When we project our envious rage onto social causes – left or right – violence easily occurs, murder and assassination become commonplace. The reification of whole classes of people follows. Intrapsychic conflicts around envy played out on a global scale show just how destructive envy can be, a fact that should persuade us all the more strongly to integrate whatever we may possess of this bitter urge.

4

Envy of the Masculine

Cinderella can go to the ball only if she finishes the task of sorting her seeds. Thus differentiating good from bad and securing a moral sense must precede meeting the prince. A basic and secure feminine identity connected to the good must be established first. Her stepmother plots to trick Cinderella, to make the task impossible. But Cinderella does the job, with the help of her good mother's spirit, symbolized by a bird, suggesting that facing ambivalence and persecution requires reaching all the way back to the goodness we have known, even if we have lost it. The spirit of goodness is available to us even though its tangible presence is not. Holding on to whatever little bit of goodness we know can open the door to more, as indicated by the godmother's whisking up of beautiful clothes and shoes and a carriage with which to go to the ball.

A woman in analysis was startled to discover that when she could admit and feel little crumbs of good things in her life, she then remembered more; goodness did not shrink but expanded. "How much?" was replaced by her looking at "What's there."

One way to read this tale is as a description of a conflict within a woman between two contrasting responses to the masculine, and between putting together or pulling apart the poles of the masculine and feminine within her. Related to this understanding is the effect on her own feminine identity of a woman knowing love with an actual man. The contrast between Cinderella's and her sisters' responses to the masculine strikes the reader as vividly as the contrast in their ways of relating to the mother.

The sisters relate to the prince the way their mother treated them: he is a self-object, chosen to enhance themselves; he is not a real other in his own right. They look upon the masculine as a prize to be schemed and cheated for, stolen if necessary. They would even sacrifice their relation to each other if it would gain them the prince, would cheerfully mutilate themselves to possess the man. In the grim parable of evil which is the slipper scene in version after version of Cinderella, the sisters hack at their toes or heels in an effort to squeeze into the shoe. They castrate themselves to get the nobleman and what they think he might bring them. But the blood dripping from their wounded feet betrays them. Their maimed self exposes their deceitful reality. Found out, they fall into disgrace, or worse in some versions, where the bird, associated with the dead mother of Cinderella, pecks out their eyes. The good persecutes and blinds them in their parody crucifixion.

A similar theme resounds, though on a more hopeful note, at the end of the related tale of "One-Eye, Two-Eyes, Three-Eyes." Two-Eyes, the Cinderella figure, gives her sisters to keep for their own the magic tree with silver and gold fruit originally bequeathed her by her fairy godmother. But the fruit simply rains down on the sisters, hitting their heads with its metallic hardness, suggesting that the source of good is theirs potentially, but that they are still in wrong relation to it. The good persecutes them. And it is inedible. The fruit image also has sexual implications, suggesting that one effect of spiteful envying is to harden a woman's sexuality and make it fruitless. Envy dries up both body and soul.[34]

Cinderella's sisters show the sad sexual plight of the enviers. Feeling so empty of goodness in themselves, they lunge violently at the men outside them or the animus figures inside them, trying to fill up that emptiness. The envious woman seizes on a male to substitute for her own unclaimed femaleness. She wants what he has, or what she thinks he has: his power, his position, his sexual organ and whatever it may represent. She reduces him to a part-object – his penis and the symbolic meaning she assigns to it – and fails to see him as a man, or herself as a woman, either of them as a whole person in his or her own right. Envy castrates both sexual identity and power, making neuters of all, male and female.

Lacking durable relation to goodness taken in from her mother that, among other things, would secure her sexual identity as a woman, the envious sister cannot take into herself the goodness the male organ represents, nor give to it lovingly. Failing to receive the penis, she wants one of her own. She envies it and all it symbolizes, and wants to tear it away, to steal it for herself. She wants to substitute the prince's maleness for the deficit in her own femaleness.

She may avoid her own emptiness by blaming it on the man – saying that his and other men's treatment of women makes them inferior, second-class citizens whose goodness has been stolen by men. Or a woman of this kind may avoid her own emptiness by trying to become the man and to possess whatever powers she attributes to him. Here her own masculine part, her animus, steps in front of her feminine ego and turns her into a pseudo man. Functioning properly, the animus would connect her ego to unconscious contents within her psyche and give her a basis within her own psychology to identify with, so that she could then understand the men in her life. When this inner function must carry her outer adaptation, however, it wreaks havoc. Hazy ideas, emerging from unconscious sources, now substitute for personal relatedness to a given situation. The woman often then appears as the worst possible caricature of the male – pushy, insensitive, substituting force for relevant connection.[35]

Cinderella's sisters always appear masculinized and unconnected to their own feminine centers, especially when seen in contrast to Cinderella's graceful femininity. The contrast is ingeniously dramatized in the witty characterizations of the men who play the sisters' roles in Frederick Ashton's choreography for the Royal Ballet version of Prokofiev's *Cinderella*.[36] Their parody femininity – ugly, whiny, melodramatic, wonderfully clumsy – captures the plight of women when their masculine and feminine parts compete and conflict. Rather than support each other in their insecurity, they argue over who will get more strawberries, jewels, or whatever from their mother. They refuse every opportunity to learn what Cinderella does naturally, always protesting "Unfair!" They eye the prince avariciously, never with any identifiable sexuality. To them he is simply a trophy to be won, to be stuffed into their howling emptiness.

Such emptiness in a woman goes back to the original vacuum in the relationship with her mother. Failing to feel fully fed and supported by this principal female – and all her surrogates – she becomes an adult woman who mistrusts and competes with women and envies men. Not fed with goodness by her mother, a little girl will turn prematurely to her father.[37] It is not so much out of readiness or love for him as it is to escape the frustration, rage, and envy she feels toward her mother, who in her fantasy possesses all that is good and refuses to share it. This hastens the onset of Oedipal feelings and lays the ground for future sexual complications. She may, for instance, grow into a compulsively promiscuous woman because her vagina has become a hungry mouth trying to take in from men the rich provender she feels lacking in herself. The hunger she feels leads to a confusion of orifices and genders to fit her uncertain identity.[38] A woman may, for example, be compulsively attracted to men who are already married or involved with other women, because unconsciously she must repeatedly rob the mother who never fed her. She may shun relationships with her own sex, relying excessively on the male in her life, whether father, husband, or teacher, artist, thinker, or movie star – whomever she sets up as arbiter of her fate, defining what she will become. She remains a blank, however, and her arbiter must fill in the content, usually from his own unconscious image of what he needs a woman to be, his anima. This sort of woman will appear on the surface as much more feminine than a sister, for example, who has taken on the masculinized role in the family. But underneath, both are ill-defined and undeveloped in their personalities, both dominated by the masculinity they try to substitute for working out who they are as women.

The implications for others of failure to work out and claim one's sexual identity are developed with a grim fullness of detail by the British novelist L. P. Hartley in *Facial Justice*. Published in 1960, it is an addendum to Aldous Huxley's *Brave New World* and George Orwell's *1984*, with a fine fairy-tale capability about the events that follow a third world war's atomic holocaust. Big Brother is now Big Sister, in Hartley's dystopia, but she conceals her sexuality behind a shrewdly chosen male voice. In a world of egalitarian futility, people are classed as Alphas, Betas, and Gammas, but the pious hope, dinned into the populace with microphonic fervor, is that all will be equal. What is more, they will be seen to be equal – women especially – as a result of plastic surgery. Women will be flattened in their Beta masks, thickened in their buxom bodies, made aggressively healthy. All of them will be, if the Voluntary Principle and Free Will so carefully nurtured by the Voice have their intended effect: "The second letter of the alphabet is best."

In fact, the crucial letter is E, for there is Good E (Equality) and Bad E (Envy). In a world where the people are addressed as Patients and Delinquents and the newspaper is called the *Daily Leveler*, where the flowers one possesses must be plastic so that they do not outshine anyone else's, women are particular threats to Good E because they are such unmistakable fomenters of Bad E. If anything in a woman's face, say cheerfulness, "excites a single twinge of ... Bad E, then it must be stamped out." To keep women in place, Betafication is best, but there are ancillary devices. One of the most effective is to name them all after murderers, classical, biblical, historic.

From the Bible come Jael, Judith, Jezebel; from the hallowed performances of the ancients, Clytemnestra, Electra; from the French Revolution, Corday. Men are not denied the distinction: we have a Brutus and Cassius, a Joab, a Maybrick. But men are not the special object of the envy-hating dictator, a natural Beta, whose sexual identity is not revealed until the last pages of the book, with her telltale sign a heart-shaped birthmark just above the heart.

The irony of *Facial Justice* is hardly concealed. In the service of ridding the world of envy, it is envy that reigns. In the drive to make everyone equal, human differences confront everyone. A splendidly ironic review of a concert, in which the same music is played by two different pianists (Brutus and Cassius, to be exact), makes the point:

> It was the mistakes and the worst-played passages that pleased me the most, for I felt in them the strongest evidence of our common humanity – that is, our liability to err –, and my resentment grew against Brutus and the flawless performance by which he had separated himself from us. Crash! Bang! With each deviation from the music my heart rejoiced, for this, I knew, was the way I should have played it myself.... Darling Dictator, blessed be his name who does not require of us more than we can give, more than the least of us can give! Long may he live to make the New State safe for mediocrity![39]

The slogan of the New State might well be "Some are less equal than others," with the central effort to make almost everyone feel a part of the "Some" who are less equal. The ugly old-woman dictator, with the egregious supply of hearts, trusts her own sexuality so little that she must be represented by a man's voice and live a veiled existence that will masculinize her for her subjects. It is not strange that in her dictatorship the family and the home are questioned as a matter of official policy and that motherhood and childbearing are suspect. She is a woman without parts, outer parts or inner parts. With someone else's virile voice and a benevolent rhetoric, she is performing a ritual of castration upon her people, reaching back beyond living generations to efface those who sired them – mothers especially. The implications for our own egalitarianism are clear. The envy that denies fundamental sexual distinctions dictates only one kind of equality, the equality of failure.

A woman caught in early envious relation to the mother cannot differentiate between the various ego and animus parts of herself so as to be in a position to put them together. This haplessness of the envied sisters, in contrast to Cinderella, is very clear in the tale. Cinderella is able and ready to join up with the prince, to unite the masculine and feminine parts. The sisters are neither clearly feminine nor content to be women and have no earthly idea how to relate to the masculine, as is humorously and poignantly shown in the revulsion, or at best kindly tolerance, the prince shows for them. His relation to the sisters is devoid of any sexual electricity or sense of meeting of minds or souls. They would neuter him as quickly as they do themselves. They cannot meet the prince at his own level, but must approach him childishly as if he were a piece of candy to grab. Churlishly, they see it as his fault that they are not happier, because they fantasize that it is within his power to whisk all their troubles away.

The sisters have no earthly idea of what it means to be their own persons and to relate to anyone really different from themselves. They are caught up in their uncertain relationships with their mother, who displays the all-in-all, male-female duality of the primordial archetype. They feel unfed by her and chained to her. They cannot get enough from her to establish their separateness of being and must put all their energy into struggles of dependence upon and defense against her. And so the mother retains her primordial identity, holding the masculine well within her, and the sisters cannot differentiate their own contrasexual part and thus achieve relationships with men or even with their own unconscious.

On a personal level, a girl's or a woman's projection of her image of masculine reality is an essential support in her making contact with men. She attracts to herself, and is attracted by, males who concretely embody what she grasps imaginatively. On an archetypal or symbolic level, a woman's images of the male and what he represents convey intimations to her of that other half of herself. These images pull her toward the union of the halves into a whole, into what Jung calls living from the self as the center of the whole psyche. These images evoke in her a longing for spiritual wholeness. They are tremendously powerful, opening her in body and soul. For the images of a man's sexual and spiritual parts are not objects a woman can concretely possess, like the parts of her own body and soul. She can know them only imaginatively and in the space of relationship. Thus images of masculine power or receptivity, of wisdom or dependence, of insight or seeking, live in her as a potent fantasy, in images of her own apprehension of an essential other. Somehow she understands that these parts of life fit together with corresponding parts in each sex. The images live as something shared between herself and the other – an actual man or her own inner maleness. They are never entirely integrated into her internal ego-identity, nor are they exhausted in an ongoing relationship with a man outside herself. This contrasexual part of hers can be claimed only if shared with another, as an inner bridge to deeper self, or outer connection to a man she loves. Cinderella is ready to live such a connection, but her sisters are not, for they are still struggling to secure an initial foothold in being, separate from their mother.

One of envy's most devastating effects is to halt this development.[40] The contrasexual archetype never gets differentiated from the primordial mother figure. It simply does not emerge enough to be projected outward and then introjected again, a process that must repeat itself many times in the course of one's relating to members of the opposite sex, refining this part of ourselves, so that it can effectively perform its bridging function to otherness. Instead, the contra-

sexual part of the sisters – their archetypal masculinity –
remains mixed up with their female identity, breeding unconscious envy of the opposite sex and conscious confusion about
their own sex. The result: the man-woman nature of Cinderella's sisters. The paths of subsequent confusion are numer-
ous. A woman may project her unclaimed femininity onto a
man and appear to be seeking a sexual relation with him,
though she may actually be trying to find in him a good
mother who will help her discover how to be a woman. Or, she
may displace the cause of her confused femininity onto him,
accusing him and all men of always devaluing females and the
feminine.

The real-enough prejudice in society against women aggra-
vates this displacement. A woman's despair over ever achieving a right relation to her feminine identity intensifies in the
face of rejection by men and exclusion from full social,
economic, and political equality. But envy between the sexes,
we must see, goes back to childhood. Male envy of women
stems from a deep level of fear of the overwhelming power of
being unconsciously associated to the female, for men who
feel prejudice against women have never grown up in relation
to their own unconscious. The mother archetype remains in
its original nondifferentiated mixture of primordial male and
female elements. As children, we register this primordial
plenitude in a fantasy perception of our mothers as all-in-all,
possessors of a penis as well as a vagina. Only gradually do we
differentiate our perception and see her as unmistakably
female, with a masculine quality carried well within her
feminine identity and expressed outwardly in her relation to
the father, himself an unmistakable male, existing in his own
right. The distinct male and female couple replaces the infantile monster image of the male-female combination.[41]

But that early fantasy persists in the unconscious and
resurfaces in the fear of the adult male who has not come to
terms with the feminine part of his own psyche, the anima.
Instead of differentiating the feminine part so that he has
some knowledge of its characteristic effects upon his moods

and behavior, and especially with women, such a man remains unconscious of it and hence all the more victim of its conditioning influence. The anima itself remains mixed with the mother image and may exert a threatening influence on a man's ego, as if to drag him back into infantile helplessness. To combat this fear, he needs to see and to put women in inferior positions, reassuring himself that he is not a small child dominated by a big mother, not a tiny ego ruled by an overwhelming unconscious that appears in the image of the overwhelmingly big mother.

Such a man may fear and envy a woman's reproductive capacity to conceive life, and then all by herself to become *the* source of food. He may need to combat and denigrate that capacity by rigging cultural attitudes, rituals, and employment practices that leave women at home, reduced to housewifely and child-tending proportions. The female life-creating gift has been envied often enough in the past, and imitated. Witness the ancient priests and shamans who wore a woman's clothing, as if to put on with it her magical powers. Sadistic crimes against women, rape in particular, betray a deep envy of fertile breasts and wombs that must be eradicated.[42]

A man out of touch with his own inner feminine part will particularly fear and envy a woman who strongly wants to develop all of herself, as wife, as mother, as contributor to her world through profession or job. Such a woman is too powerful in the eyes of his unconscious; she has it all, penis and vagina. She already possesses the potential to reproduce life. If she also achieves power in society equal to men and can produce the cultural and spiritual life necessary to human survival, she threatens to dominate. Therefore women must be paid less, promoted less, depotentiated in every way.

Only a man comfortable with his own anima can welcome a woman who wants to be all of herself. Only he can willingly seek her fulfillment. Lacking connection to his feminine part, and projecting it onto women for them to carry, he fears and envies the female as his overpowering enemy. He feels dependent upon her in an infantile way and feels his adult self-image threatened. The male-female, mother-father archetype that he projects onto women symbolizes the fullness of being itself and its creative power. Fear of this amplitude of raw power and the shame of failure to build a durable and conscious relation to it underlie the root hatred of the female. The woman who receives such a large-scale projection inevitably is discriminated against in a determined effort to seize what she symbolizes from her, to keep it from her, insulated, segregated. It is one of the maddest of all the fantasies unloosed by envy, to believe that being itself really can be controlled by one sex.[43]

The mother archetype dramatizes both the power and the fear of being. It is identified, as Mary Williams suggests, "particularly by the capacity for orgiastic excitement."[44] This excitement is a body symbol for the joy of being and its sheer vitality, the pleasure and goodness of all its parts performing together in an ecstatic whole. But such an image of pleasurable joy can be too threatening if we have disowned goodness. Rather than work at putting together our male and female parts, and integrating our dependency in an ego strong enough to experience its origins in a strong person of another sex as a suitable devotion to a reality beyond itself, we simply turn away from the good.

We can see now why envy follows so closely upon pride at the pinnacle of the seven deadly sins. We refuse the good and its joy, turning to bitter emptiness instead. Too often we find ourselves particularly distrustful of women whose directions and enthusiasm in any way suggest a sexual ease of proficiency as, in her own curious way, Cinderella does. We are ourselves more at ease with the glum or violent temperament of the ugly sisters.

The collective significance of the envious sisters' position speaks to any social movement whose members fail to value their individual differences and to acknowledge that they themselves make up the parts and pieces that must be put together, to make a working society. Envy of someone else's differences, while at the same time forsaking one's own differentiating reality, produces the temptation to force a totalitarian conformity on all members of a social grouping.

In contrast to her sisters, Cinderella is ready to meet the prince as a person in his own right, not as a substitute for her own self. She faces the envy that assaults her, tackles such tasks as sorting the lentil seeds, and welcomes her fairy godmother's help. Cinderella deals directly with her own reality, and all sides of it, bad and good. She is ready for union with the masculine. She does not use the prince as a detour away from her own self.

The prince stands for the missing masculine parts in this fairy tale. The story opens with four females and no males and ends with a male-female union that reorders relations among the females. To begin with, the stepmother and sisters envy Cinderella, thus defining the tale's psychological problem – how to get right relation between the female parts where good is not dominated by bad. The story reaches a climax with the appearance of the fairy godmother who makes publicly visible at the ball the warmth and openness Cinderella has nurtured in herself. The decisive pitch of the drama – the midnight deadline, Cinderella's disappearance, and the prince's search – concludes with a happy union that signifies the redeeming of the devalued feminine standpoint by Cinderella. Envy does not triumph. Goodness does, with an acceptance of masculine elements (her animus) by Cinderella, with the promised joining of the masculine and feminine parts within her, and by symbolic projection, within all women who can claim their full sexual identity as she does.

The masculine prince, the next ruler of the realm, can be seen in a symbolic way as standing for a woman's coming into right relation with her own authoritative governing power. How will the feminine ego join up with the masculine part of her psyche? How will a woman unite with a real man? On what basis? Coming from deficit and envy – the sisters' position – means annexing the masculine for a woman's own purposes, not relating to it as a genuine other. The shoe will not fit. Coming from a real self – Cinderella's position – means a woman really opening to receive the masculine, not to annex it or to be consumed by it, but rather to unite with it, as equal with equal. The shoe will then fit.

Cinderella represents the woman who comes into possession of all that belongs to her. To do that she needs her masculine part, a need that is symbolically indicated by the fact that her shoe is made of glass. Glass is hard and breakable, and does not conduct heat or cold. It is isolating. Yet one can see through it; it does not cut one off entirely. That Cinderella's foot is enclosed in glass suggests more needs to be done for her, that she may need greater emotional warmth, perhaps, something to make her still more human and flexible, not at all brittle or isolated. Sometimes a hero must break glass to free a maiden, climb a glass mountain to liberate her from bondage. Here the prince himself must put the shoe on the maiden's foot, the shoe originally bequeathed by the godmother, suggesting that even connection to the archetypal good through magical powers is not enough. The good must also be grounded, stood upon, walked in, incarnated in human emotional relationship, and specifically one between the sexes.

The slipper stands for many things: wholeness, healing, a sure fit. Its precise size, which will accommodate only one foot, emphasizes the individuality of standpoint needed to support a person's own authority and experience. Though we share many things as human beings, each of us to some extent stands apart. Each woman, then, must find her own particular place and means of standing in herself and in her world.

The slipper is among other things a sexual image of a female vagina encasing a phallic foot. Here, too, the emphasis is on a special personal relationship. For the shoe will fit only Cinderella and no one else. And the prince will know her only by the shoe matching her foot. This detail stresses an important fact: a woman must establish a particular personal relationship to her own sexual organ and sexuality. She must feel claimed and recognized, called out from femaleness in general, to be her own special woman, by her own special lover.

He, too, must know and claim *her* particular sexual organ, *her* body, *her* person, seeing her as unique among women, one utterly herself. But he can only find her when she has tried to find herself. He must then hunt for her specifically, and go over all the kingdom to find her. If she remains anonymous to him, submerged in the collective categories of lover, wife, woman, union does not occur. Only when her particular personal being, and her particular sexuality, with all its idiosyncrasies, become the woman for him, his specific and intimate other, is union between them possible. The same matching holds for a woman within herself, if we interpret the prince as an animus figure to whom she makes connection. The prince may also symbolize a male's ego trying to find the missing feminine part of himself, that jigsawlike piece fitting deep down inside him, where his personal standpoint is expressed by his anima.

The prince cannot find Cinderella without help from her. This is the kind of help that means hard work for a woman's ego. She must consciously inspect who in fact she is as a woman, what her sexuality, her body, her emotions are, and she must stand firmly with those. The matching of foot and slipper offers an image of a woman's psychic task in putting the male and female parts of herself together into a functioning unit and in the right order. Her feminine organ clothes a masculine ability to take a stand. Her feminine identity surrounds her masculine part, carrying it into the world, suggesting the right relation of an ego fully open to its animus.

The spirit of a union of these parts, both within a woman's psyche and between a man and a woman, is what love is about. The man loves the woman's vagina, her sexuality, her person. She knows in his love the ultimate validation of the desirability and worth of her femininity. But only she can make possible such acceptance of herself. Cinderella knows who she is, knows that she is the one the prince loves, but he does not know it until she puts her foot into her slipper. A woman needs to reveal her true self, to show her person, her ego parts, her animus parts, her sexual parts, and how they go together, before a man can recognize her. Indeed, in most of the versions of Cinderella, either she takes the shoe and puts it on her foot, or the shoe jumps out toward her foot and slides on, or she brings its mate out of her pocket. Then the prince can recognize her. He needs her to do the self-revealing act so he can find what he wants. The animus depends on a woman's ego to show what it needs and wants.

The validation of a woman by a man occurs only after a woman's own validation of herself as a functioning ego animus, and female-male wholeness shows that she appreciates herself in rags as well as in ball gowns. She must accept her vagina and her phallic potential. She must know she is a person who longs for union with another person. She thus validates both her sufficiency as a woman and her desire for completion by a man. Best of all, she knows the reality and the goodness of the desire she feels.

The inner union and the outer can occur only when all the parts of self and other are brought together in awareness. Cinderella's goodness consists in her wanting to bring all the parts together. This is a heroic feat of willingness to own all that belongs to oneself and to risk longing for what is beyond one. In contrast, the envious sisters break into fragments, drop parts of what they are and try to steal the parts they miss from others.

Cinderella does not cover up her shabby dress but shows it openly, does not hide her fine slipper but reveals it boldly. She does not pretend she does not want the prince but openly displays her desire, yet she also makes him come to her, search for her, and find her in her real, not at all fairy-tale-like world.

Perhaps the most astonishing fact about the marriage that looms at the end of the Cinderella story is its refashioning of the original good-bad, female-male duality, portrayed at the beginning of the tale in terms of the mother archetype. Cinderella and the prince stand for the sorting out and uniting of these primordially undifferentiated female-male, creative-destructive aspects of the mother archetype. The mother figure embraces the opposites, but in a disorderly archaic mixture that buffets the female ego rather than feeds it.

The original duality of the good-bad bisexual mother reaches differentiated form in the readiness of the male-female parts to unite in marriage. If strong envy intervenes, however, this development will be interrupted and stalled, if not altogether blocked. For the envying and dread of the good will prevent its being separated from the bad and taken in, absorbed. The good will remain in disorder. The bisexual mother never yields to a female really related to the male part of her own identity. Failing to relate, the female remains in its primitive monster form, overpowering, frightening. Then the contrasexuality that should have developed is experienced under the sign of envy – the penis envy of females and the dread and hatred of women of males. Cinderella's sisters cannot relate to the prince; they want him and hate him, but they cannot love him.

Cinderella sorts out the good from the bad and arrives, at the end of the tale, to make a proper joining of parts into a functioning and happy whole. The power of the marriage image lies in its picture of this conjunction, the uniting of everything so that nothing is lost.

5

Envy of the Good

Cinderella and her sisters differ sharply in their responses to goodness, although both feel empty of goodness. Cinderella's mother is dead and her father absent and she is constantly exposed to the persecutions of her stepmother and sisters. The sisters, lacking a father, have only a negative mother who conscripts them into her power plays. They feel a corroding resentment toward Cinderella. But here the similarities cease. For Cinderella directly, openly suffers her loss of the good. She allows herself to feel her hunger. She weeps her sorrow. She wishes for good. The sisters refuse to experience their emptiness. Instead they hurl it in accusations of blame onto Cinderella. It is her fault they feel awful. They deny their own suffering and to the extent that they acknowledge its existence at all, turn it into someone else's malevolent doing. They flee their own being. Their hunger as a result can never be appeased, because it is never fully admitted. Fury replaces the suffering of that lack within themselves. Good, which is being, is responsible for their bad, which is beinglessness.

Cinderella stays with her being – her experience of hunger for the good, her desire to be filled up. Out of this being, even though it is painful, arises a doing that brings her close to the good. Cinderella longs for the ball just as earlier she longed for love and nourishment from her departed mother. She holds to the good she has and wants more. She does not deny her emptiness any more than she denies her partial fulfillment, as far as it goes.

What is so hard for envious people to accept is the good they have known, however small. They are overcome by their emptiness and make it even emptier by throwing from awareness the small fulfillments they do possess. Cinderella shows us the right attitude. She can still desire and reach toward what she does not have while holding on to what she does have.

The sisters, in contrast, disown their being, cover their hunger by false feeding, getting Cinderella to run here and there for different foods and dress and service. They pretend they are not hungry, not empty and miserable, insisting on their superiority. They dread admitting their desire for the good and dependence on it. Out of that dread springs their pseudo doing and persecution of the good. They take offense at it, deny its reality, hide from its presence, and are certain they will never be given anything.

Denial of the good quickly leads to hatred of the good. The pseudo doers of the world, determined to keep hidden their dependence upon those who really get things done, put themselves in the paradoxical position of hating something – goodness – which they deny even exists. The effect is maddening. One of its results is scapegoating.

The suffering servant is always the ideal candidate for the role of scapegoat. He or she – incarnate God or fairy-tale figure – has an immense dignity that cannot easily be dismissed as mere pomp or the clothing of high office. The servant seeks neither power nor position. The very weakness and shabbiness of the servant is his or her strength. There is simply no mistaking the authority of a Jesus in his setting or a Cinderella in hers. They stand as constant challenges to those around them for whom the only affirmation is denial, to whom the unassailable goodness of suffering servants is an open invitation to perform every possible violence upon them.

The goodness of the servant is unassailable, but the physical person is not. What begins as envy ends in ritual violence.

The suffering servant becomes a class or race of undesirable, unwanted persons. A systematic metaphysics of class or race warfare follows, justifying every form of segregation and, ultimately, of extinction. The theoretical statement is followed by more practical treatises remaking whatever is necessary to support the metaphysics – in history, anthropology, economics, psychology, or theology. Then after a suitable interval, trial, imprisonment, and execution follow.

In the nineteenth century and earlier, the time between the assertion of the theory and the translation of it into physical violence was fairly long, long enough to make escape possible. That is one reason why in earlier times there was such a large number of suffering servants in exile, and mixed with the true servants of goodness, such a quantity of pseudo servants who could develop their own metaphysics and warfare of envy from the safety of their banishment. In this century, the gap between theory and practice has been closed. Holocausts come quickly. Concentration camps are prefabricated. A gulag archipelago can come into being almost as spontaneously as an earthquake or a volcanic eruption.

Of course, the spontaneity of an earthquake or volcano is a surface effect. That sort of destruction has antecedents that reach back into prehistory – perhaps, if the enthusiastic rhetoric of cosmologists is correct, billions of years back. The scapegoating to which envy often leads also has ancient roots, primordial in fact. The dread of the good is at the very center of human evil and is in some ways the most puzzling of all the elements of the mystery of evil. But some parts of it, as with all the great mysteries, are clear. Wherever our allegiance may be in the camps of philosophy, whatever our theological position, we cannot easily deny the fact that dread of the good means dread of being. Those who stand so firmly in these ranks, not simply against goodness but utterly opposed to those who are good, are shaken by being itself; they fear it as intensely as they do death.

Those who are against goodness and thus against being, the great deniers for whom Cinderella's stepsisters are exemplary, are not as a result eager for their own extinction. Far from it. It is the death of others that their envy covets. They cannot take up their own being with any satisfaction. Why, then, should others do so well with theirs? The politics of envy follows from this: Do unto others what they would not do unto you.

What makes this position so terrifying in the modern world is that it is so heavily buttressed by theory, so total in its violent reach across the differences of human personality to being itself that it becomes an unshakable creed and way of life. Negative affirmation rules all. The *cogito* formula becomes, "I envy, therefore I am," or "I hate, therefore I am." And this visceral conviction comes to replace the motivation of being. Those who live by it live only by shunning the good where the good is most pronounced, in those who exemplify it. They live, as Cinderella's sisters do, by suppressing the lives of others.

Cinderella, in contrast, actively seeks the good. She not only longs for it, but goes out after it. She misses her absent father and opens herself to love, without any guarantee of finding it. In theological terms, she corresponds to the good given her by gratefully accepting the gifts of the fairy godmother. That is precisely what the envious person finds hard to do. As one patient said, "I want the analysis to work and I don't want it to work, because you might get credit for it."

Cinderella uses her energy in the right way. At no point does she engage in a toe-to-toe struggle with her enviers. She goes about her business, looking everywhere for the good. When it comes she accepts it and enjoys it. No masochist, she. She is a receiving woman, who welcomes being and goes out to meet it. She loves the silks, the jewels, the golden coach and liveried footmen. She eats at the ball. She dances. She responds to the prince. She takes her chances wholeheartedly, without measuring, without trying to guarantee their outcome. She shows herself in finery and accepts admiration. No false modesty, no hiding in the corner, no swelled head.

She wants to meet the prince, and having met him, wants to love him and receive his love. But not at the expense of her real self. She returns to her rags and gives up any reliance on magic, in order to be seen as she really is, in all her parts, including the lowlier and dirtier parts of her personality, the bad alongside the good. The prince must find her *there*. Still, when he does come to find her, she steps out to be found; no hanging back, no sniveling excuses. She accepts his claiming of her and gladly joins him in marriage.[45]

In some versions, Cinderella, while still the mysterious beauty at the ball, shares the goodness that has come her way with her envious sisters. She feeds them oranges, which she knows they particularly like. This detail in the story portrays a potential turning point for the sisters and for the envying side in all of us that they represent. They take the food from Cinderella because they do not recognize her. She has never really been seen by the sisters, who can barely see themselves. It is no wonder, then, that they admire this beautiful princess who actually does see them. They marvel at her goodness in sharing herself with them, thrilled that she notices them and gives them fruit. Here the sisters change their relation to the good for a little while because goodness is presented to them from a great distance, far enough away so that they can accept the bare fact of its existence and allow it to deal with them. They do not see the value of the envied one until she comes as a stranger and a mystery. Then their admiration for the good pours forth. Cinderella's transformation occasions their own, and for a little while they feed on it.

This kind of shift in being must occur in the envious person: a shift from the resentful questioning of being, "Who has the good instead of me?" to a forthright: "Where is it? Let me look at it! Let me take it in!" It is almost as if the good has to become depersonalized, more abstract, more general, a mystery we share in common rather than one person's possession, before enviers develop admiration for it in place of their dread. They need to disidentify from the good as a personal possession, even if it is one they lack. They must recognize the good as a reality in its own right. For the envied, however, this does not last long. Cinderella is discovered again by her sisters after the ball. They hate her once again just as much as before. Even Jesus, who kept saying: "Why do you call me good? I am not good. Only he who sent me is good," could not unseat lethal projections. With him their full potential knew realization: his enviers put him to death. But goodness was not killed; resurrection followed.

Goodness is never killed. Resurrections of one kind or another always follow the violence that claims a suffering servant as its victim. We have much to learn here from the primitive societies that built their order and very survival upon the transformation of violence into a sacred ritual. Whether through deliberate sacrifice of life, human or animal, or the use of sexuality or drugs, one way or another these societies recognized the need to shelter and concentrate their destructive impulses. They saw, sometimes with full consciousness of what they were doing, that order could be established and continuity be assured with the use of a real or symbolic victim. The language of the ritual might speak of the appeasement of the angry gods, but clearly what was being assuaged was the anger of the people themselves – and more than anger, the bloodlust, the greed for power, the need to control the elements, the drive to feel a new strength within themselves and the hatred and envy of those who seemed not to have their need nor to feel anger or greed.

We do not have to emulate the violent sacrifices demanded in primitive rituals to share the insights that provoked them. We can come with something more than mere curiosity or intellectual titillation to our anthropological inquiries. We can look for the enduring truths that are thrown back at us when we stir the primordial waters. Perhaps we can come to see the wisdom of the primitive cultures that understood the feelings of ordinary people when confronted by those extraordinary men and women among them who were not consumed by anger or greed or their own weakness in the face of natural catastrophe. The wisdom resides in their recognition that one way or another the strength of the suffering servant would have to be gathered up, taken in, and shared by the rest. We may find ourselves horrified still at the solution – the sacrificial procedures – that this wisdom ordained. We must not as a result lose sight of the wisdom itself. For the truth remains: we must still find a way to take in and share the strengths of our suffering servants. The failure to do so does not bring an end to violence, ritual violence or any other. Now, instead of the sacrifice of one victim, real or symbolic, we have genocide, in which symbolism plays no recognizable part at all and the only certainty is that millions of people will be killed.

Each of the massive conflicts of the twentieth century has had as its excuse the promise of an end to such conflicts, and in each case violence has prepared the way for more violence. In spite of all that we have learned – or at least thought we had learned – in modern anthropology and psychology, we still approach each of our wars and revolutions as if it were merely political or economic. In spite of what should be the most convincing evidence of all – endless carnage, destroyed cities, concentration camps – the nostrums remain the same. Change the politics. Reform the economics. Make over society by giving the people power. How? Through Congress or the Supreme Soviet or the revolutionary tribunal that will rule when the movement – whatever the movement may be – takes over. As if power can be legislated or passed on by committee decree. As if sheer desire, once organized into the rituals and rhetoric of a movement, can be satisfied simply because it has been organized. Are the rites of primitive societies so much more senseless by comparison? Is even an abominably treated scapegoat in such societies to be compared to the scapegoating of whole peoples?

We cannot return to the precise procedures of primitive societies for all sorts of reasons, not the least of them the fact that in our peculiar civilization we are made queasy by the deliberate killing of a single victim. And yet we can somehow live, after a momentary discomfort, with holocausts. No, we cannot return to ritual sacrifice, but we can make good use of what we know about the violence that still lives within us. Unacknowledged, it effects its own sacrifices, finds victims all over the place with remarkably little difficulty. Faced, as it is some of the time in the rituals of psychotherapy, it can be put to some valuable use. If we make the connection between the internal violence of envy, for example, and the external savagery it causes, we can move some of the way toward containing it and giving its energies positive purpose. We can gather up the strengths of our suffering servants and share them. But we must do so with full consciousness. Otherwise our goodnesses do not survive in us as they must. We postpone our resurrections at a terrible cost.

In Cinderella's case, we do not know the outcome for certain. In one version, the sisters overcome their envy to take the goodness Cinderella offers in bringing them to live with her at court. In other versions, they undergo transformation of their attitude to the good. Two-Eyes' sisters, for example, can keep the magic fruit tree to help them learn a more loving attitude to their sister, now their future queen-to-be. In other examples, the sisters' envy destroys their sight. The good mother's spirit in the form of a bird pecks out their eyes, suggesting they have lost the capacity to see the good and all possible insight into it, knowing goodness only as persecutory. In an analysis that fails to heal envy, it is painful to see goodness clearly offered and equally clearly refused. The envier goes hungry and the one who wants to nourish is left helpless.

6

Treatment

What can we do in the face of envy? No blueprints exist, no guaranteed formulas. But approaching envy from the standpoint of the envied one can show us concrete steps to take. The envied one proves to us that, finally, the most appropriate response to envy is to look to the good, to understand that goodness will bring our parts together with each other and with being.

Being envied is to experience someone wanting to tear away part of oneself, or failing to do that, to spoil it utterly. The envier says in effect: I will steal the goodness you display because I want no part of the badness in which I feel confined. I will put that badness onto you and accuse you of trying to escape it, saying you refuse to deal with the bad. I will steal your good by saying you refuse to deal with the bad. Then I will replace you as owner of the good.

The envied one can learn from this attack the full plight of the envier – and just how awful it is to miss a central part of oneself. For envy is the attempt to break everything whole into parts, to fragment an as yet undifferentiated unity. In that destructive energy lies envy's catalytic power to lead to its transformation into something positive.

The envied one learns that no solution emerges from trying to persuade the envier that no injury was intended and no good withheld. The envied one discovers that disowning the good only makes matters worse. And then the envied one may learn how good it is to get a missing part back and to go out and help others retrieve their missing parts too. For goodness means being willing to take what is and hold it together and willing other people to bring all their parts together. Goodness, like poverty, we always have within us. For in both cases, being is prized for its intrinsic value. Whatever Cinderella's ultimate destiny, she must experience poverty. It is her training ground in being, her tutoring in the multiple parts in which being comes to us.

Goodness recognizes that we do not come into the world with useless parts. The whole point of the Cinderella tale directs us to this insight. Cinderella is seen as a rag, burnt up, with her discarded parts thrown away into the ashes. But this refuse, when gathered together, turns out to be good. She puts her parts together, however awkwardly. She wants to reconstitute a whole. She looks for any possible connection and thus becomes the emblem of goodness she is.

The first concrete step we can take to recover a lost goodness is to reach to the place where it was lost and where dread of the good began. A personal, durable, and enjoyable taking in of the good must replace the envious spying of it in someone else and the despairing losing of it in oneself. Where offense was taken in the good, a gratitude and sharing in it must somehow now occur as the Cinderella story teaches us and the experiences of psychotherapy confirm. This movement from the negative to the positive is the pivotal force in treating envy disorders. It can only work if analyst and patient reach to the envious emotion that has blocked the patient's development. Repair of the ego-self axis, first experienced and damaged between mother and child, will take analyst and patient directly into the thickets of envying emotion, much as in the drama between Cinderella and her sisters.

In such encounters, the analyst most often gets cast as keeper or withholder of the good, assigned the role of idealized envied object, emptied of personal reality. One patient, so much in distress she kept calling the analyst at home between sessions, was unable to take in the analyst's words or presence on the phone because of her envy of the idealized family life she attributed to the analyst, triggered by the sound of music in the background and the voice of the analyst's husband when he answered the phone.

The envied analyst may be caught at first in defending against this depersonalization by all the temptations that beset the envied one. They are many: overeagerness to relieve the patient's misery that may result in excessive interpretation, premature disclosure of personal foibles as if to disown the idealized goodness being projected onto the analyst, discouragement over failures and subsequent withdrawal, or a giving way to impulses to retaliate against the patient's envy by relentless reductive analysis. All these responses mirror the patient's own reactions to the tormenting envy.

On the other hand, the analyst may play an omnipotent role to defend against helplessness or may identify with the patient's projection of idealized good onto him or her as a defense against the patient's hateful attacks of envy. Putting on an air of perfect goodness, the analyst becomes invulnerable, out of reach, too good to be true. But then the analyst's inflation will aggravate the patient's envy, as he or she plays all-good to the patient's all-bad, seeming to be all-understanding, which totally confuses the patient, being all-kind and fully occupied, apparently without need, which simply intensifies the patient's angry, distressed emptiness.[46] The analyst thus acts out an unconscious sadistic retaliation against the patient's envy.

These are merely ways of staying out of the difficulties the analyst and patient must inevitably and even appropriately fall into if the blockage around envy is to give way. Envious emotion simply must be allowed and acknowledged as present in the analytic relationship. Like the ancient alchemical process that sought to dissolve fossilized objects into their primordial fluids, an analytical relationship must submerge both the rigid, idealized good and the persecutory bad back into the turbulent currents of the patient's hungry love.

From such a return to an undifferentiated state, distinct parts may emerge that the patient's ego can take in, even if only one bit at a time. For this to happen, the analysand must again feel the hunger that envy expresses, the need for something beyond the self, the longing for contact with a good given rather than self-produced, the yearning toward a good altogether outside one's own control. Feeling these needs, desires, longings, hungers, and yearnings opens a patient wide to a vulnerable state, breaking down the hard defenses that envy has given rise to and thus making reception of the good once more a possibility. The analysand again experiences the hungry need that envy had concealed. And that helps break up the primitive state of the psyche – the fusion of ego and self – into separate parts.[47] Goodness means putting parts together, not just happening on a ready-made perfect whole. That is too idealized a procedure, for it comes at the expense of the patient's participation. Consciously feeling envy, by contrast, hastens the emergence of these parts. We contribute to goodness by finding the emerging parts that belong to us and trying to piece together all that we find, just as we do the work of evil by discarding the parts or refusing to bring them together.

The analytical task focuses on sorting out which level envy is operating on at a given moment, like Cinderella's sorting the edible from the spoiled seeds.[48] For to reach to envy's initial impulse of hunger for the good releases an envier's vigorous appetite for the good, which is the exact antidote to dread of the good and effects a turning toward it once again.

The second concrete step toward recovering the good and dispossessing envy demands that both envier and envied reach to the archetypal background of the emotion. Envying and being envied are then revealed as two sides of the same coin, two opposites out of which a third uniting attitude may emerge. Idealized good splitting away from persecutory bad is just the situation of Cinderella and her sisters. Missing from both is a good-enough good, a durable and accessible good. In the treatment situation, both analyst and analysand must cross over to each other's opposing emotions, so that eventually the envious patient can feel the Cinderella side of the conflict and not stay stuck with her unfortunate breed, the envious sisters. It was Cinderella's willingness to feel her emptiness that made it possible for her to be filled with the good. Feeling this kind of attraction to goodness will move a patient to a new departure point, for beneath the malevolent attacks stirs an eager, even aggressive wanting to take in the good.

The patient accomplishes this reaching to the Cinderella half of the envy experience by showing an unabashed yearning for the good, no longer hiding the desire in rags. It is a change of attitude like that of the sisters when they see and cannot help admiring Cinderella in her beautiful clothes at the ball. This change sets the patient the next task: to find personal connection to the good, recognized now as in one's own sister, that is, as a real part of one's own personality.

Similarly, an envied analyst must cross over to play the role of an envious sister and experience being emptied, without any personal good. The analyst suffers some of what the patient does – being seen as a child appropriated to the needs of an envious parent. In the transposition of roles, the analyst feels in relation to the patient as a child does under a parent who takes the child's accomplishments but rejects the child. The patient-turned-parent appropriates everything the analyst offers while discarding the analyst himself like a banana peel.[49]

Another route by which the analyst may assume an envying sister's role comes as a result of the analyst's strenuous efforts to recognize in himself the experiences of envying the patient. Harold Searles gives a poignant example. He worked nine and a half years with a severe and chronic schizophrenic patient. Progress occurred only when Searles brought to consciousness repressed feelings about his patient: "These feelings included intense envy of his inherited millions of dollars and of the various forms of contentment his hebephrenic mode of living afforded him," such as lying about smoking all day. Searles also confesses feeling envy for a female patient, once grotesquely ill, now recovering because of Searles's labors. As she improved, he felt "overwhelming awe and envy of her healthy-young-giantess quality, her Junoesque quality, her quality of radiating an innate social superiority to me. On such occasions, I would feel personally, in contrast to her, overwhelmingly puny and socially inferior, and would have no sense whatever that I had made any contribution, however small, to the improvement in her."[50]

Still another, perhaps less obvious way an analyst can come to recognize envy of the patient occurs when the treatment takes a spurt forward with the appearance of powerful new images or deeper insights within the patient, and an increased firmness and clarity of connection between analyst and patient. Here the analyst may jump in with excitement, either wanting to proclaim the progress, explain its meaning, or insist on bringing in details from his or her own personal life as a way of sharing the experience. The analyst is displaying the impulse of Cinderella's sisters, lunging after anything new that may appear on the scene, hogging center stage, and thus stealing the analysis from the patient. Though the theft may be unintended or unconscious, the analyst appears to be demanding from the patient all the good stuff – all the attention, energy, praise, and admiration. The analyst seems enviously to be gobbling all the good, and whether trying to do so or not, once again making himself or herself into an enviable object.

The third concrete step to be taken to heal envy is really to recognize the other – envied or envier – as a subject in his or her own right. Envy always makes people into things. Healing envy restores both envier and envied to human form.

The envied one is often tempted the same way the envier is – to see the other, the envier, as nothing but a devil bent on persecution. That is to take him or her too personally. Cinderella, after all, never asks what she did to cause her sisters' envy. She sees the envy as emanating from them, not as caused by herself. The intense negative scrutiny of the envier must be reversed in the positive gaze of the envied one, firmly concentrated on the envier's personality and situation. Paradoxically, if the analyst takes a patient's attack personally, the patient will become depersonalized, lost from the analyst's sight. By looking at what a patient is experiencing, the analyst feels the envious attack as what it really is, more or less impersonal, motivated by the envy of the patient, not by any failure of the analyst. The envier is almost always simply hungering after the good. Envy is a primitive recognition of real quality in another person. Only too quickly we sneer at it. If both analyst and analysand can see through the sneering to the hunger beneath, then envy will act as a catalyst for the development of the envied good.

To effect this change in envy, we must be sure it is firmly located in the envier. That, we must remember, is where it arises, not in anything the envied one does or fails to do. Envy creates its own targets out of its own nothingness. It always flares out of emptiness or a lost good. For example, a woman with a career suddenly falls victim to her married sister's envy after that sister's last child has grown up and left home, thus ending a major part of her sister's life as a mother. In her loss, she spies her sister's fullness and envies it. A male patient discovers that he is blocking out what his analyst says because he envies what he sees as the analyst's magical ability to know what is going on and to communicate it to him. His action loses the analyst's help and leaves him empty.

An analyst can speak directly to that emptiness, however, and locate the source of envy precisely where the patient feels it – in his or her lack of something. This returns the envier to his true subjective state, to an emptiness that he can now feel and acknowledge. The same man now says he feels very sad to realize he wants to hurt the analyst precisely because he knows the analyst can help him.

This is envy experienced at the level of hate, with a shadow component of real desire to injure the giver of good. It is important for the analyst to identify that component and for the patient to feel that hate as a personal emotion that actually connects him to the analyst. The envy is thus contained within the personal relationship between them. The patient is not left alone with his hate, nor is the hate treated as some impersonal urge. The patient feels it as a connection, even if a negative one, with a true person. Eventually, in a relationship that is well established and making progress, a patient's hate will yield to sorrow and guilt over his wanting to injure someone he needs and admires. Envy thus acts as a means of development. Allowed to be felt in its hating stage, it will be transformed into concern for its effect on the analyst. The patient thus comes to encompass his envy within his great feeling for someone outside himself.

The analyst, as the envied one, gains the stamina needed to survive this hate only by holding firmly on to the envied qualities and not allowing the emptying out that an envious attack intends. The analyst must learn from examples like Cinderella's, holding to the good, not by identifying with it, but by pointing to it, admiring, making it available the way Cinderella gives fruit to her sisters at the ball. Then the patient will come to look at it this way too. For example, a woman who consistently complained at the end of every session, often in tears of despair, that "nothing that was any good happened today," came at a later time to cry tears of sadness when the sessions ended because what had happened in them "had tasted so good." She wanted more. But she did not feel the reality of her desire until she first felt her hunger. And she did not feel her hunger until the analyst firmly and repeatedly said that good things had happened in the session and were there for her to take in.

Such a patient cures an analyst of any hesitation about holding to the value of analytical work and developing good feeling as well about a patient. One learns as analyst that not holding on to good qualities destroys any possibility of an analytical connection. What an analyst does as an interpreter is less important than going on, living openly with the positive qualities, and pointing to their availability in the work and relationship with the patient. "Helping" and "doing" responses have to give way to "being." Then a patient can relinquish the grabbing, attacking, spoiling, envying tactics, all the various kinds of negative "doing," and experience the "being" of hunger and genuine desire for the good.

A *fourth step* occurs as a result of seeing the other as other, as subject and not object in an internal drama. Goodness existing in itself emerges as an other between analyst and patient, "dwelling among them," to borrow New Testament words. It emerges from the ashes, freed from being either person's servant or possession, to be attacked or withheld. When the analysand feels a hunger for the good and does not identify it as a lost possession nor one stolen by another, but lets the good be, it can be found in the relationship. When the analyst holds on to the good and does not identify with it, its archetypal nature emerges more clearly as a transcendent reality, existing in its own right. This brings great relief to both analyst and analysand, because positive qualities can be relied on to be there and do not have to be acquired or managed as one's personal property. The envied one does not have to fear assault and robbery and the envier does not have to feel withheld from, intentionally deprived. Goodness is there between them for both to feed on.

But this recognition of the objective, transpersonal existence of the good happens, paradoxically, only through the most personal and subjective connections. As in the mother-child relationship, analyst and patient must learn how to connect to each other's temperaments and idiosyncrasies. Facial expressions, body postures, pauses, intonations fill out the particular textures of their unique relationship. They reproduce between them the tensions, positive and negative, of human relationship at the source, in the first meeting of persons with their mothers.

On the analyst's side, the wording and timing of interpretations comes to be fitted to the patient's particular rhythms and appetites, exactly as a sensitive mother responds to her new child. On the patient's side, tolerance, and even fond appreciation of the analyst's quirks, must come in time to accept the ambiguity of a mother's nourishment, sometimes fully available, sometimes necessarily withdrawn. Both come to trust the goodness that flows between them as nourishing their present relationship as much as it repairs past deprivations in the patient.

The woman who cried over the end of the good session came to the next one with a new willingness, even an assertiveness, to take the good she found there. The analyst was in an adjoining room before the session began, but had left her office door open. The patient, coming early, entered and sat down. When the analyst arrived, she said: "I found your door open and came in. If you hadn't left it open, I would have waited, but you did, so I did too."

There really can be fairy-tale-like denouements in the analysis of envy. They do not guarantee a living happily ever after, but they do offer the immense relief that must come when reality is identified and confronted and goodness is seen to be a central part of it.

The last concrete step in treating envy has to do with seeing the good and feeling gladness in it. Taking it, one risks enjoying it and really sharing it. Envy serves once more as a catalyst for a startling development, in the same way conscious acceptance of envy can break down defenses and release hunger for the good, and feeling the hate contained in envy can yield guilt over hurting the other and can stimulate the wish to repair the damage done. As deep and searing as is the suffering envy brings, if consciously admitted and suffered, it can act as an agent of profound psychic transformation. Balm does come out of Gilead. Saving truth does emerge from a dark and lowly stable.

Envy can lead one to take gladness in the good if envy is felt all the way down. For envy, after all, is admiration gone sour. But admiring the good must come first. At the bottom of envy is a lavish, all-out sighting of good qualities and registering of awe and amazement at them. What is this glorious thing? It seems so wonderful, so grand, so present, so *there*. Only in the cruel instant that follows do we concentrate unhappily on the place of goodness there, in someone else, not here in us. Only then do we chafe and object and say with Cain, Why you and not me? Experiencing envy to the dregs, all the way down to the underlying hunger and admiration that envy masks, will open us again to a presence of goodness that will quicken our souls with gladness. We must then yield to the energy of the good and allow its sheer exuberance to burst through without embarrassment.

Goodness is not weak or timid. Goodness does not smirk. It is our unwillingness to trust our own good feeling that makes it emerge in such cautious and affected colors. We must rejoice in our sense of the good with at least as much intensity as we bring to our envy. Then we can share our good feeling gladly with others. Patients wanting to give gifts can be seen this way sometimes, as eager to share gladness in the good. Some deeply need to share their delight in getting better. A moving example of this emerged after long treatment of a highly disturbed woman, who slipped in and out of persecutory and hallucinatory fantasies. She was just able to keep a minimal job, and her fee for treatment was very small. After a number of years she finally felt able to take a promotion at work, no longer having to reject it as in the past for fear of envious persecution in retaliation for her self-assertion. Her salary increased a tiny bit. Triumphant and glad, she insisted her fee be raised. She wanted the analyst to share in her success. She needed to feed another out of her own new abundance. Though the raise was small, the analyst felt, and continued to feel over many years, the richness of her gift. Gladly taking in a good thing that happens always leads to sharing.

The Cinderella tale makes the same point. When Cinderella and the prince find each other, the whole kingdom is enriched, and not only with a new king and queen. Their joy in each other eddies out to include the entire realm in celebration. This suggests the collective importance of individuals trying to come to terms with their dread of the good, to take it in and enjoy it. The parts brought together inside and outside – ego and animus, woman and man, ruler and subjects – bring many things and persons together. That fitting together is felt as joy. Goodness does feel good. It does exist among us and does lead us to trust and depend on each other.

Thus, in contrast to the beginning of the story, where goodness is lost, fought over, made into an abstract ideal and dreaded, the end result is personal relation to a good-enough good and a substantial sharing in it. We do not have to be or do it all. We can depend on others to supply what we lack, and be glad for their abilities and talents, for together we make up a whole, and a desirable one.

Parts can be put together in this way because goodness existing among us this way is not the possession of any one person. Thus opposing envier and envied, persecutor and idealized object, possessor of the good and dispossessed, no longer need be pitted against each other. The opposition dissolves. We are free to face the multiple guises of goodness, which is at least as complex a presence as evil and a far more fascinating one when faced with appropriate courage and delight.

If we take Cinderella and her sisters as a group picture of an inner conflict within a woman, we can see an end to the war between ego and shadow parts over who owns the good. No one part does. The ego disidentifies from its possessing role and the shadow gives up its spoiling tactics. The good will be shared between them, facilitating the growth of cooperation and mutuality, not just between these parts of the psyche but also between the one woman and other women in her life, those onto whom she has projected her shadow. Typical dream motifs that turn up in this transition will feature either the figure of a woman's shadow, that previously robbed her, now offering to share things with her, or an entirely liberated shadow figure, treating her with unmistakable kindness. As bits of goodness are taken in and enjoyed, envious parts surface more easily and can be cared for and assimilated. As the envying parts are experienced, the good that is available can be seen better and taken in and enjoyed, even if only in bits. A benign and enlarging energy is set in motion, greatly weakening the destructive power of envy and freeing it to transform the psyche by pointing to the available good.

As the power of envy weakens, the original, massive, bisexual, undifferentiated mother image, which is the first image we have of the unconscious, begins to break up into parts, allowing for the development of the contrasexual archetype. Envy has close connection to our sexual identity and much to do with our relations to the opposite sex. If holding to the good and taking in bits of it is not achieved by the ego, the contrasexual image is not sufficiently differentiated to be projected onto the opposite sex and then integrated. An image of the opposite sex that will act as a mediator to the ego of unconscious contents is not formed. The ego remains in the original mother-bound condition where it can only envy the opposite sex its organs as the prerogatives of unachieved adulthood.

A woman's ego is stuck either in the envious sisters' position, seeing good things as always in the prince's power and always withheld, or in Cinderella's position, feeling under constant attack just for longing for such things. The sisters remain trapped in their mother's negative orbit, never finding their own center. Cinderella, in contrast, performs such tasks as sorting the good seeds from the bad, and makes the long journey from loss of the good to building connection to it. In her, the contrasexual image can develop. She and the prince present each other with the clearly differentiated masculine and feminine elements originally undifferentiated in the mother. And in their unmistakably distinct identities they find their container: What they have in common is their differences.

The close connection of envy to the opposite sex and the contrasexual parts of a psyche shows up in analysis at each specific phase of a transference. Usually, a positive connection to the analyst must be established before the patient can risk transferring to the analyst the envying parts of his or her psyche.

A sturdy container is needed before the acid of envy can be released into consciousness. There may have been much unconscious acting out of envying impulses up to this point. The decisive fact now is that envy can be admitted and experienced with open awareness of its pain and destructive intent. Because there is enough confidence in the goodness of the relationship, the patient can risk projecting and then looking at the envious parts transferred to the analyst. This is always an anxiety-inducing process, because envy so grossly distorts reality and, when consciously experienced, makes a patient feel slightly crazy. For example, one woman alternately experienced her analyst as a fine feeding source and as an envying woman who wanted to thwart realization of the patient's power and sexuality. At those moments, she put onto the analyst the intent to keep all the power for herself, never sharing any and seeking to blight the development of the patient's abilities. This woman was able, through transference, to get a look at this fearful inner attacker – which did in fact prevent her from developing her considerable talents. But it was heavy going for both analysand and analyst to look at the ruthless emerging force. It linked the patient to her own contrasexual part, her animus, which needed development so it could convey to her ego much-needed energy to fulfill her ambitions. Up to this point, those ambitions were alive only in fantasy, and could not be brought to realization. The unconscious expectation of a massive envy attacking her, and from the very source of nourishment she depended on, prevented her from accomplishing what she wanted so much. She felt unfulfilled and a failure. She was convinced that if she used her talent, she would be cut off from the food on which she depended. To her, it was as if her mother were rejecting her precisely because she was developing and using her own thrusts into the world.

In a similar way, issues of sexuality – the ability to give and receive pleasure, for example – constellated envy in the transference. She experienced the analyst as wanting to steal her sexuality, to package it according to some abstract formula.

This felt like theft and a depersonalizing of her actual experience, forcing it into conformity with what the analyst or the
analyst's system needed it to be. Again the analyst had to carry
the attacking force of envy until both could look at it and see
how it undermined the patient's sexual enjoyment. Then she
could find access to her own sexual energies and enjoy them.

With male patients an issue around envy and the contrasexual anima usually turns up after secure establishment of a
good relation between analyst and analysand. The man begins
to see the different parts of his psyche and the plenitude of his
unconscious reactions, emotions, needs, hurts, and dream
figures. He feels himself floundering, not knowing how to
connect to all this and make use of it. A previously tight and
controlling ego attitude has given way to a more receptive one,
but he does not know how to go on from there. At this point,
transference of specific anima functions may fall onto the
analyst, who no longer carries the image of the mother or the
totality of the unconscious.[51] Now the analyst becomes the
connecting link to the unconscious, the one who can focus
and present the parts in some relevant order to the male
patient's ego. Initial envy of the analyst as containing everything, as carrier of the unconscious, gives way to reliance on
him or her to carry the specific anima function which puts at
the disposal of a man's ego different parts of his unconscious
life. Exploring the transference of this anima function to the
analyst builds up in the man his own ability to use and
respond to the parts of his unconscious, and thus returns to
him an increased sense of his own masculinity. Less and less
is he childishly dependent on a great mother to provide the
necessary sustenance. More and more he feels in touch with
feeding sources within himself which will make him receptive
to the needs of others. The decrease of envy allows the
increase of his anima function.

Thus the image of the loving couple at the end of the fairy
tale may be seen to symbolize the inner marriage of parts, in
both a woman's and a man's psyche, as well as the right match
of man and woman. The healing of envy leads to a proper

joining of ego and contrasexual parts. For the contrasexual image holds out the good in appropriate form, a goodness one can join with, penetrate, and receive.

This vision of marriage as bringing together the male and female parts of the self accounts for its tremendous power. Beneath the social value of marriage as a stabilizing institution that harnesses sexual energy and provides protection for the young lies the spiritual dimension of marriage. This is where the making of a whole person out of the inner parts is externalized, where a whole connection between persons is effected, where a whole kingdom takes shape. The whole that goodness constructs is joyous, not simply healthy, alive, not merely functional.

We are called beyond ourselves into each other while we are confirmed, each of us, in who we are separately. Reaching the contrasexual image is the necessary prelude to reaching goodness. It is a putting together of all the parts, including the discarded, the envied, and the envying, those which feel the same and those which feel otherly, the male and the female. The male and female parts symbolize all the different kinds that we can find and put together. Goodness is something we keep building and yet never finish. There is always something new to be found in the otherness that brings us together.

The way to have being, we must learn, is to share it. The experience makes us feel glad, grateful, generous. Thus the Cinderella tale ends in collective happiness. The whole realm is renewed. For central to the gladness is the happy awareness that we can rely on others, because we share our condition and only together can make it thrive. Vying, robbing, envying, spoiling occur when we feel estranged and separated into competing parts. Fitting foot to slipper, joining the parts into a whole, a differentiated whole put together with a mosaic solidity, is to experience grace.

Another way to describe the experience is as a nourishing trust. We trust the endurance of the good, despite the attacks of the bad, because we have fed on it. We trust its presence, flowing deep in us, keeping us alive.

Part Two

Theological Explorations

Introduction

The wisdom of the fairy tale is the wisdom of values. It draws much of its narrative energy and many of its actual chara ters and events from the excmplary tales of the Middle Ages and the moralizing fables of antiquity. The fairy tale is, like so many of its sources, unblushing in its value judgments. In it, the encounter with evil is direct, even savage, as guardians of the tender sensibilities of the young have noted. But equally, goodness is bold and as firmly identifiable as the bad. No one need wonder for long in a fairy tale about which are the good guys or the bad guys.

We take sides quickly enough, then, in our reading of fairy tales, and not only in our first reading, as children. Young or old, we remain fascinated by something more than the violence that so often afflicts good people, whole towns of them on occasion. We are caught even more when goodness triumphs, when something larger than the defeat of a villain is accomplished. A value has been served. Our confidence in the possibility of goodness, even in a world of ogres and witches, is supported. And what is more, the perspective in which we discover and identify both the values and our confidence in them is equally psychological and religious. We come to accept, through the wisdom of the fairy-tale imagination, the many-sidedness of the human psyche, its propensities for good and evil, for self-affirmation, self-denial, and self-

destruction. We see, both in the conflicts and in their resolu-
tion in fairy tales, the substance of religious concern. Human
fallibility makes such immediate sense in this setting that the
melodramatic rhetoric of sin does not seem so exaggerated.
Human love and kindness are made so appealing and persuasive here that the heightened language of faith does not seem
so distant from the colors of the world we inhabit or so
uncomfortably unctuous as we might have thought. If we
think about it for a moment, we recognize in these terms the
kinship of fairy tale and our dream experience.

It is hard to say which more properly serves as explanation
for the other in this theater of values, the dream or the fairy
tale. Both work extremely well to make our unconscious lives
accessible to us. Both feed the religious imagination, which
lives on allegory, fable, parable, and mystery, and finds its
special joy in brief, clear, stimulating tales with endless possibilities of interpretation, such as that of Cinderella. When we
bring together the ancient insights of religion and the clinical
understanding of depth psychology to elucidate these simple
stories, we discover how well we have been endowed from
childhood with materials with which to make sense of ourselves. The most strenuous experiences can be faced. The
most frightening of our nighttime or daytime phantoms can
be looked at. We stand up, supported by all the suffering
servants, to find value in the midst of misery. We are rescu-
able, the least of us, the most downtrodden, as in all the fairy
tales. But just as in those tales, and in the tortuous corridors
of psychotherapy, we must be willing to confront whatever or
whoever turns up. When we do, we will find we can take on
even such formidable opponents as envy and do so with value.

7

Envy as Sin

Just as the perspective of depth psychology throws new light on our experience of envy, so a religious perspective illuminates the background issues that make envy such a devilish trap. It is much harder, for example, to heal a patient's unconscious wish to defeat treatment when that wish results from envy than when it springs from a superego that demands punishment for every success. Such a superego presupposes a set of values existing in the patient, values that can be modified, whereas envy points to a gaping hole in the patient's personality, where no one has yet come to be.[52] The traditional religious notion of envy as sin illuminates what that gaping hole is and its destructive effects on the self.

At first glance, envy seems to differ from other sins because they each point to a goal in itself not evil, except when indulged to excess. Gluttony is hunger gone wild, for example. Lust is sexual desire run rampant. Anger is self-assertion enraged. In contrast, envy presents itself as feeling demeaned by another's good fortune and wanting to belittle the other's good to protect oneself. Envy wants to make something alive into something dead. Envy looks hard for evil in another person and takes great satisfaction in finding it. On closer inspection, however, envy reveals itself as more, as fierce attraction to the good at the same time that it resists the good, a wrestling finally with God, the source of the good.

Envy, like the other fateful failings, did not secure a place
on the list of cardinal sins until Gregory the Great in the
seventh century.[53] But Scripture refers to envy as a recognizable and treacherous emotion. The Philistines envy Isaac
(Gen. 26:14). Rachel envies her sister (Gen. 30:1). Joseph's
brothers envy him (Gen. 37:11). The psalmist counsels against
envy (Ps. 37:1), and Proverbs advises against giving way to it
(Prov. 24:1, 19). The deadly effect of envy clearly is feared:
"Wrath killeth ... and envy slayeth" (Job 5:2); "Envy is the
rottenness of the bones" (Prov. 14:30); "Who is able to stand
before envy?" (Prov. 27:4). The Hebrew word for envy, *qin'ah,*
means a burning, the color produced in the face by deep
emotion, reflecting sorrow that others have what we want.
The Greek *zeros,* zeal, in its envious form means carrying
things to excess, being inconsiderate of self as well as other.
Phthonos, another Greek word for envy in the New Testament,
characterizes the unredeemed life and the spirit that crucified
Christ (Matt. 27:18, Mark 15: 10).

Envy, understandably, has few proponents, however many
may be secretly enlisted in its service. For Aristotle, one of the
first to give it its place in a systematic examination of moral
behavior, envy is intrinsically evil. It has no neutral zone for
him, as, for example, anger does. Envy clearly condemns a
man because it is so untouched by what either the envied or
the envying really deserve.[54] And Aristotle's reasoning is followed, with suitable variations to allow for time and place and
temperament, by almost all who take it up, almost always
briefly, as if to say, 'Let me rid myself of this poisonous
substance.'

For Spinoza, envy is "hatred itself," the pain one feels in
another's good fortune and the pleasure one may take in the
other's suffering. Hobbes is content to array envy alongside
emulation in his spearing of the appetites of *Leviathan:* we
merely emulate when we join our *griefe* at "the success of a
Competitor in wealth, honour, or other good ... with Endeav-
our to enforce our own abilities to equal or exceed him"; when

we assuage the grief with our attempt "to supplant, or hinder a Competitor," we envy.[55]

Hume follows Descartes in classifying envy as a passion and recognizing some of the psychological constraints that lead to it. He sees the special pain for men in watching their "inferiors ... approaching or overtaking them in the pursuit of glory or happiness." And this we feel particularly strongly in people close to us in character or social rank or profession.[56]

Though envy is for Descartes a vice and "a perversion of nature," he sees some excuse in the passion that arises when the "less worthy" possess a good that we seek, as long as we confine our hatred to "the bad distribution of the good which we envy, and not to the persons who possess it or distribute it." Only a rare form of generosity and justice will counteract the hatred we feel in such situations. But understanding this, Descartes must also insist on the misery of envy – "there is no vice which so detracts from the happiness of men" – both for those who feel envy and for those with whom they share their bilious company. He is punctilious about the medical details as he has observed them: envy properly enough is called *livor* in Latin, which means a leaden color, "one of mingled yellow and black like battered blood," an effect Descartes says he himself has observed.[57]

Whether or not the envious can always be discovered by their livid color, they are a sad lot whose spiritual complexion is unmistakable. The 1967 Catechism of the Dutch Catholics, famous for its tolerance and warmth, has very little to say about envy. The definition is only too clear and the color only too evident:

> Possibly the ugliest and most abhorrent of all sins is envy – to be vexed at seeing other people being happy. This is really a sin against life. As the saying goes, people go green with jealousy – the colour which is most in contrast to the complexion of health.[58]

The language in Thomas Aquinas' *Summa Theologica* brings the whole tradition together, from Aristotle through the seventeenth- and eighteenth-century philosophers to the moderns, without the color of either medicine or literature. Envy is one of the vices opposed to charity, taking its place alongside hatred and "sadness touching spiritual and supernatural good," and ranking with "discord within the soul, wrangling and fighting, schism, strife, sedition, warfare." It is a sadness, like the distaste for spiritual things which Thomas discusses in this same dismal category, and it occasions even in his dry text a tincture of compassion. A mortal sin that yields "numberless" other sins as one tries to avoid it or to follow where it leads, it sires, the Summist tells us, "obloquy, detraction, gladness in the adversities of our neighbour, affliction at his prosperity, and hatred."[59]

The only kindly light in which the sin of envy can be observed is that in which, upon occasion, the envied can see those who envy them. The story of "The Envier and the Envied" in *The Arabian Nights* stresses this. There we see the victim of an envious neighbor, who pushes him into a well to die, not only forgive the envier but heap honor upon him and wealth and position. In the well, the envied good man is befriended by some genies, who instruct him in a cure for his Sultan's daughter. She is afflicted with "Madness," inhabited by a bad spirit. The good man rises from the well and finds the white hairs of a particular black cat with which to dispossess the girl of her devil. Inevitably, then, he marries the princess and succeeds to the throne. What is not at all predictable is that he will send for the sinner who dispatched him to the well and, without explaining why, in effect reward the sin.[60] The inference is ours to draw: sin may prove an occasion of goodness. How so? In the sense that it brings us right up against the nature of good and evil, of being and nonbeing, of creature and Creator.

To recognize envy as sin places it within the movement of original sin, as a falling away from the good, as a choosing against what is offered. In Judeo-Christian tradition, being is always created being, its goodness found in its essence as given being, as being connected to its author, God. Evil is a falling away from that author, not seeing what is, focusing instead on what is not – seeking a being as divorced from its source and its dependence. Thus evil is experienced as an active depriving of being *(privatio boni)* as well as of goodness, for goodness is essentially being as created being.[61] Sin is evil experienced within the boundaries of this primary relationship of creature to Creator, even if recognized negatively as boundaries to be broken.

In envy, we do not focus on a specific goodness in another's being. Nor do we focus on the actual desire evoked in us that may activate the development of a matching goodness in ourselves. Rather, we focus on a missing quality – the absence in ourselves of what we spy in our neighbor – or we concentrate on our wish to obliterate that same quality in our neighbor, to make the something that is there into nothing. We fall away from spontaneous admiration to ruminate on what does not exist or on how we can extinguish what does exist. Cinderella's sisters whine about what is absent, not what is present. They want to smash Cinderella because of what they do not have.

Sin involves will. It is an active urging against the existence of good, whether in oneself or another. For that reason, in exploring envy as sin we begin with the envier rather than the envied. Envying reflects our despair of ever getting hold of the good.

Approaching envy through the experience of envying allows us to examine the effects of envy on the envier and to find an analogy in the suffering of the envied one to the plight of the good. We begin with the sisters' position and move to see Cinderella as a female Christ figure, hardly divine, but a true suffering servant and scapegoat. For it is the good that the envier refuses, a refusal that skews the relation of Creator to creature, that is always mirrored in the relation of envied to envier. In both, relation to the good is broken because a basic orientation to being has been falsified. Recovery of connection to the good depends, finally, upon repair of that fundamental tie to being that has been wounded. To effect a cure, we need to recapitulate the whole wounding experience. We must move from investigating the effects of refusal of the good upon the envier to the fate of the good itself.

8

The Envier's Spiritual Plight

The envier's refusal of the good produces devastating effects on everyone's spiritual integrity. The envier refuses the goodness involved in simply being the creature he or she is meant to be. The envying do not want their own person but someone else's. They want to return the being with which they have been saddled and substitute a carbon copy of someone else's.

When we envy we are not willing to find and live with our own self, with all the hard nasty work that that involves. Instead we want to seize another more glittering self. We may severely damage other persons with this violent thrust at their being, but even more seriously, we refuse what is our own. We hunger and desire to be a person of substance, but we are unwilling to nurture the only substance we can ever possess – our own. Because ours is so dim to us, we seize on what others have that is clearly visible and try to grab it from those who did in fact welcome it and give it room to grow. In our unwillingness to accept what is really our own, we do not want the other person to have anything either. So a piece of music or a poem another has written becomes a mere product to be imitated, no longer an expression of a whole human life struggling to articulate a vision. A beauty of face becomes no more than a surface appearance, a fashion to ape, never a presentation of a particular self where face and clothes mirror soul. A talent becomes an acquisition, a means to power, ease, or fame, no longer rooted in a person's way of life or express-ing multiple and subtle choices and sacrifices to develop particular gifts.

We see another's good as divorceable from the other's being, not created by it. We want to take it and run. That is why envy produces shoddy work, shells without cores. The terrifying acceleration of envy into increasingly indiscrimi-nate habits of attraction, drawn only to surfaces and quick sensations, shows envy spinning ever faster away from a central core of being.

When we envy we almost always miss what is our own, for we are never at the place where we are but only where the other is. Moreover, we see others falsely, distorting them by reducing them to their envied parts. We come toward others with someone else's self, one we have concocted as our version of the good, never meeting the other in our own person but only as the person we are imitating.

The refusal of ourselves strikes a major blow against our spirit – that center of our integrity as unique and original persons. However damaged or undeveloped we may be, the spirit is the core of our integrity in being what we are equipped to be. That core falls into shadow when we envy because we ourselves pull away from it, run from it, in fact, in our haste to take on the trappings of someone else. We are unwilling to take faith in that being which is ours, choosing it for itself, for ourself, claiming what we have been given. We flee it by setting up obstacles, wanting what another has instead, or a whole host of others. We can avoid thereby what we have been given, by focusing on what we lack.

There is no more precise description of a man setting up obstacles to his own goodness than Dostoevsky's *Notes from the Underground*. The Underground Man, a forty-year-old "public servant," keeps a scrupulously exact record of his life *iz podpolya*, from "between the floorboards," as the title should read in English. He is, as he tells us at the very beginning, a spiteful man, unattractive, with a bad liver, not even up to the rigors of becoming a full-fledged insect. He does know something of goodness and beauty, but the more conscious of it he becomes the more he sinks into his mire. What particularly distresses him is the performance of a really direct man, who "simply dashes straight for his object like an infuriated bull with its horns down," and who will be stopped only by a wall. This is the normalcy he yearns for: "I envy such a man till I am green in the face." He may be stupid, but "perhaps the normal man should be stupid.... Perhaps it is very beautiful."

Envy has made the Underground Man despair, has made him defiant of the laws of nature and arithmetic: "I dislike those laws and the fact that twice two makes four." And so he tries to sink further and further into his own degradation. He confronts his colleagues with his detestation of them. He sets himself up for a duel with a lofty officer, but his hopes for a dramatic encounter are reduced to a mere bump in the street. He struggles to make those around him over whom he can lord it – his servant, a prostitute – share his despair. But he fails at everything, at the bad as much as at the good. He cannot withhold his servant's wages. For all his insulting treatment of her, Liza the prostitute moves toward him "with an irresistible impulse ... yearning towards me." She finally throws her arms around him and bursts into tears. "I, too, could not restrain myself, and sobbed as I never had before." All he can say is: "They won't let me.... I can't be good!" He knows that he hates her and is drawn to her at the same time. That much he knows, but not much more. As he has said of his shadow existence, "There are things which a man is afraid even to tell himself."[62]

The underground life of envy is a constant theme in Russian literature, not always identified by name, but just often enough to make the symptoms clear. The flight from being is unmistakable. The epidemic power of the disease is terrifying to contemplate. We see it in the conjunction of ambition and sloth in Gogol's Chichikov in *Dead Souls*, the model of all the petty figures of officialdom. His plan is to acquire a monopoly in the brisk market for serfs who have died since the last census but whose names are not yet recorded as dead. Using them as collateral, he can build himself a fortune. He almost succeeds, but as the macabre title of Gogol's book proclaims, fortunes built on a sloth-filled envy can produce merely dead souls. The only energy available to a Chichikov is for flight, and the book ends with a famous run from justice in a speeding troika. What is simple justice is that Gogol's manuscript is incomplete, his own ambitions for his novel and for his country left where they should be in such material, in mid-flight.[63]

Eighty years after *Dead Souls* and sixty-three after *Notes from the Underground,* another Russian officialdom, another sloth-stoked envy, was chronicled by Yury Olesha. His picture of life in 1927 Soviet Russia is called, with a directness that the Underground Man would have admired, *Envy.* The work confused Soviet critics almost as much as Soviet officials. It was at first greeted with enthusiasm as a portrait of petit-bourgeois hangovers in a revolutionary society. But ordinary people found themselves too much in sympathy with Olesha's antiheroes. The world of envy described by the enraged brother of a food industry commissar was only too recognizable to readers:

> Envy is gnawing us....
> Yes, envy ... one of those grandiose dramas in the theater of history which for a long time evoke the crying, the raptures, the regrets and the anger of humanity.... You are a clot of the envy of the dying epoch....
> The heartburn of envy is horrible. How oppressive it is to envy! Envy squeezes the throat with a spasm, squeezes the eyes out of their orbits.

The book had to be denounced and withdrawn, finally to be brought back into print with cautious acceptance after the death of Stalin.

Olesha's world is a world of mirror inversions in which Jesus' first miracle is reversed by an unknown citizen at a bank collector's wedding. He has advised everyone: "You don't have to love one another. There's no need to be united," and counseled the bridegroom to desert his bride. Running away from a fight with the groom, he leaves behind him a table full of bottles of port wine which have turned into water. This is a society in which the peak of a food official's plans is to produce the world's largest cafeteria, but the achievement is only endless scaffolding. His brother, on the other hand, creates a machine that works, a "horrible iron thing" with no clear purpose, an ironic invention of Soviet Dadaism, but it works – it impales its inventor. All that is left to envy is total withdrawal. The protagonist of the short novel feels that "now the time had arrived ... the time of catastrophe. To break, to break with everything which was ... it's necessary to step over the border, and a life, repulsive, hideous, not his – an alien, forced life – would be left behind." The inventor of the machine, recovering from his caricature crucifixion, proposes a toast to indifference, "the best of the states of the human mind," and tells his companion that it is his turn to sleep with the amiable aimless woman they will share together in their communal withdrawal from communist society.[64]

Russian heroes and antiheroes alike thrive on their awareness of the attractions of withdrawal from society. Theirs is a rich atmosphere for envy and it hovers over almost all the central figures in the novels of Turgenev, Dostoevsky, and Tolstoy.[65]

The topic was alive before the novels, in the dramatic poem of envy, Pushkin's one-act "little tragedy," *Mozart and Salieri.* In marvelously precise blank verse, Pushkin gives envy its working theology, a justification by works of art.

The envy of Salieri, a competent composer and a gifted teacher, for Mozart's genius is well enough known. His hissing at the premiere of *Don Giovanni* is a famous incident. Upon that fact and the rumor that Mozart's mysterious death was the result of poisoning by Salieri, Pushkin constructed his drama. It is all Salieri's. There is no justice, he tells us in a long opening speech, neither on earth nor in heaven. He has given himself to music, at first secretly, then with open diligence, courageously throwing over all he "had loved and ardently believed" to serve his art. Fame arrived and with it peace. He was not envious, not of anyone, no matter what his success. But now – "I say it myself, now I do know envy! Yes, Salieri envies, deeply, in anguish." Where is there justice when after such service, such love and sacrifice, genius does not come to reward him but rather "puts her halo around a lackwit's skull, a frivolous idler's brow"? With that description, the "lackwit," Mozart, enters, bringing with him a blind old fiddler, whose playing of a tune from *Don Giovanni* is more of a taunting than Salieri can bear. The bitterness of Salieri's envy is intensified when Mozart plays a tune for him that had just happened to fly into his head in a sleepless moment. Salieri is appalled that Mozart could have loitered in a tavern to hear an old blind fiddler when he was bringing such music to him: "You, Mozart, are a god and do not know it. I know it."

That is Salieri's excuse for murder. "If he lives on, then all of us will perish – high-priests and servants of the art of music." And if he survives, will music benefit? No, it will fall again when he dies at last. And so, in a second quick scene, Salieri puts poison into Mozart's drink, but not before Mozart has added his own unconscious collaboration in the act with talk of death through the *Requiem* he was commissioned to write by a mysterious man in black and by a question he asks about Salieri's friend, Beaumarchais. Is it true that the playwright once poisoned someone? Salieri doubts it. Right, says Mozart, for Beaumarchais was a genius, "like you and me," and "villainy and genius can never go together."

Mozart's brief testament to beauty, after he drinks the poison, is less than eloquent. All he can say, watching Salieri's tears over his deed, is how good it is that not everyone feels the power of harmony as Salieri does: "… for then the world could not exist; no one would stoop to care about the needs of ordinary life; all would give themselves to art alone. We are a chosen few, happy idlers … priests of beauty." When Mozart, feeling ill, goes off to sleep, Salieri bids him a terse good-bye, and alone, wonders about his own gifts. Do villainy and genius never go together? What about Michelangelo?

The reference is to the rumor that the sculptor murdered the model for his Christ in order to have a more realistic basis for his art. Was that simply a story concocted by "the dull, stupid crowd"? Or was it – and this question is implied rather than spoken – the justifying freedom of the servant of art? The answer is clear. In order to justify itself, Salieri's envy must deny the real freedom of art, of beauty, of goodness, the freedom of the spirit, which, far from obliterating being, celebrates it.

Pushkin's elegant drama demonstrates with breathtaking economy, in less than three hundred lines, the crippling effects of spiritual denial. It sweeps everything aside – all standards of value, art, life itself. No matter how we see the irony involved in Salieri's understanding and esteeming Mozart's genius better than Mozart himself, no matter how much more we may be pleased by Salieri's discerning self-analysis than by Mozart's sententious testimony, we must recognize the terror of the denial of the spirit that underlies envy like Salieri's.[66]

This spiritual denial goes deeper than the psychological defense of denial, where we refuse consciousness to what we cannot accept as part of our own personality. This spiritual denial resists what we have been given to be, striking out against the very ground of our being. We deny our being as created, and hence as related to a Creator from birth until death. We refuse to acknowledge the existence of that ground by insisting on looking at what it is not instead of what it is. We repudiate our own being, which may be why envy was accounted in medieval reckonings as second only to pride in deadliness.

In psychological terms, envy effects a privation of being that sets the stage for subsequent deprivations at the hands of others. Envy stops us at the beginning, before we have really started, so that we cannot get on with becoming. Choosing against our own ground of being, we have no place to stand,

and hence we help others around us to deprive us of recognition as persons in our own right. We facilitate others treating us as negligible parts of an indistinct collectivity of persons when we deny the uniqueness of our own persons.

Others, then, will always feel the contamination of our envy, even if unconsciously, and will often, as a result, choose to avoid us. Who, after all, would seek out Cinderella's sisters as companions? When we envy we choose against ourselves, indeed actively repulse our own being. In a sense we try to rip up our roots and so all but require others to dismiss us as inconsequential.

In psychological terms, envy moves us to reject the self that lives in us, the ordering center of our whole psyche. Rejection of the self keeps us envious, and envy keeps us rejecting. Our ego's task is to build relation to this larger center of the self which acts, as Jung says, like a god image within us. We reject this self out of envy of its superior power and fullness, resenting that it makes us feel puny in our ego stance.

Like Satan, the archetypal envier, we refuse our rightful place in the order of things, choosing instead to create our own order, which amounts to nothing but disorder in the end. We want to abandon this inner god image, to leave it in the stable or hunt it down with a massacre like Herod's murder of the infants, or crucify it, because its numinosity makes us feel inferior, meager, mediocre. Or we may be moved to abandon this inner divine child, this seed of potential wholeness, out of dread that if we did connect with the energies of the self they would make us into an object of another's envy. Rather than risk that disabling attack, we reject the good as it comes to us. The symbol of Satan reminds us how truly collective our envy is, how much it is a sin we all fall into: both individually and as groups, we reject the terms of creation.

There is a literal failure of the imagination involved in the rejection of our central self. We fail to see the god image, the person image at our core. We develop that habit of refusal of ourselves which was what the Middle Ages meant by *sloth*. This idleness of the spirit may be accompanied by any number of other energetic undertakings. We may be zealous in pursuit of a career, of pleasure, of sexual fun and games. But what we are after in this case is not *our* career, *our* pleasure, *our* sexuality.

What in fact we altogether overlook or turn from is our own special qualities, our own gifts, our own kind of work or play. The identity we show to the world is a false one. We are guilty of spiritual laziness.

Envy easily leads to sloth. We seek what belongs to someone else and altogether reject what is ours. We become sluggish in spirit, losing joy, opposing joy, bearing in our hearts that *accidioso fumo* – sluggish smoke – which identifies the sullen slothful in the fifth circle of Dante's hell.[67]

The subtlety of the effects of sloth makes it easy to overlook and even more difficult to understand. That great Spanish poet of the baroque, Francisco Quevedo, himself both envying and envied, says that envy is thin because it bites but does not eat. That is particularly true of the envious slothful, made eager by their failure to feed their own being. The Greek verb for envy, *phthoneo*, includes among its meanings to begrudge, refuse, or withhold through envy or jealousy. What even the most thorough lexicons do not point out, however, is that what we begrudge or refuse may be our very selves.

Miguel de Unamuno calls envy "the internal gangrene of the Spanish soul" and finds its roots in those "superficial" people who lack "deep personal preoccupations." He means something quite different from an insistent narcissism. It is his way of defining the spiritual laziness that marks "those peoples in whom the true, intimate, religious urge, creative faith and not parasitical dogma, rusts in disuse." What replaces the sense of self is an acute awareness of another's self, as Unamuno dramatizes so well in his novel *Abel Sanchez,* where everything Sanchez possesses – family, talent, love – is the object of envy of his friend, Joaquin Monegro. Joaquin is a doctor and not in any way an inconsequential man, but he is so corroded with envy and so dependent upon it that, when Abel falls ill, he is desperate to keep him alive so that the object of his envying will continue to be available. Without the envied, the envier, who has become frigid to his own being, cannot survive.

Ice and smoke, these are the signs of envy dissolving into sloth. The slothful are frozen in their retreat from being, and yet, for all the sharp edges of their icy condition, they are indistinct to themselves, hidden from clear view in that smoke which, for Dante, crystallizes their sullenness to self. Unamuno's Joaquin seems unreachable to his wife, caught behind an invisible wall of ice, their sexual intimacy shadowed by something "sinister," the kisses offered her either filled with rage or like something stolen, neither his nor hers. Joaquin is so captured by his envy and its accompanying sloth that he must altogether refuse his own being, though he thinks he would like to survive. But how can he survive except in his hatred of the man he envies? "Ah, if I had been capable of loving her," he says of his wife, "I would have been saved. For me, she was only another instrument of vengeance. I wanted her as the mother of a son or a daughter who would avenge me.... Did I not, perhaps, marry to create other hateful beings like myself, to transmit my hate, to immortalize it?"[68]

The result of refusal of the self is not its annihilation or disappearance within us, or escape from the envy we so fear. Instead, the self goes on living in us, but only negatively, as an unlived life whose principal manifestation is the envy we hoped to avoid. For all that should live in us, but is half dead, looks enviously at the life in our neighbor. The pull of our particular destiny, which should unfold as the thread of our life's journey, instead drags after us, tangled, knotted, undelivered.

Dante's way of dealing with the negative selves who drag themselves through their unlived lives is to hurry them along in afterlife on the fourth terrace of purgatory, whipped by a zeal to acquire the grace they shunned on Earth. Here, at the precise center of the *Commedia*, in the middle of the seventeenth canto of the Purgatorio, "the love of good which falls short of its duty is restored, the slack oar is plied again." Love is the restorative. The energy to pick up the spirit is drummed up in the hurrying figures of the penitent slothful. But love was always available to these figures, as Dante makes clear in a long, thoughtful, two-canto dialogue with Virgil. We turn from love, seeking our neighbor's demeaning in order to assure our success, hating anything in which another may surpass us, imagining insult, and demanding vengeance.

The atmosphere in the center of purgatory is a turgid one. Dante succumbs for a moment to drowsiness, even after Virgil's "clear and explicit discourse." But the tumult of the running crowd of penitents arouses him. "Quick, quick!" two of them cry out, "so that time may not be lost by little love." That is the answer to spiritual laziness. We are all moved by love, by the fiery movement of the spirit which is desire. And the mind seized by love will not rest until "the thing loved makes it rejoice." But this is not an automatic movement. In our freedom, we can and often do reject it.

The rejection of love is not a trifling matter. It separates us from ourselves. It creates a break between us and God, between Creator and creature. For Dante, failure in love, sloth in this pivotal area of human life, is nothing less than a gap in creation. He creates a dynamic setting to show how serious it is and to mark the splendor that comes with the closing of the gap. He asks the reader to remember the effect of a mist in a mountainous region of such density that one cannot see except the way a mole does, through the feeling of the skin. Then the sun comes. The imagination is quickened, that imagination which fails us when we fall into spiritual laziness. This is a purgation for which we do not have to wait until the afterlife. We have always with us the quick movements of love, the darting arrows of desire. We do not necessarily respond, however. Our imagination may be lacking. If it is, we miss a grandeur waiting to be moved in us that has found its source at the source of everything. Dante makes his point, first with acid, then with nectar:

> O imagination, which so steals us
>   at times from the world around us that we pay no heed

though a thousand trumpets sound about us,
who moves thee, if the senses do not reach thee?
A light moves thee which takes its form in heaven,
either of itself or from a will which guides it downward.[69]

With enough imagination, we may be able to see ourselves in our ultimate setting – the creature as the product of the Creator. No one of us can be more than that. No one should be less. But we must possess the necessary imagination and thus the love that brings us to the heights of heaven. Thus we repair the gap in creation and answer sloth – and envy – with love.

9

The Envier's Sexual Plight

Envy strikes at the basic ground of our sexuality. If our spirit is the basic core of our integrity as a person, sexuality defines the most striking marks of our identity. Sexuality is a central part of the body's language, the means through which we reach most strongly to others, from the first "smell" of the other to the most intimate minglings. It is never a minor form of identity, a mere biological presence, simply directed to the preservation of the species. It is imprinted with the defining character of each one of us, and can be seen in gesture and posture, in all the apparatus of feeling that we keep hidden and in all the drama of expression with which we openly communicate our feeling. It is visible, too, where we have been slow to recognize it, even after all the undressings of the so-called sexual revolution, in the individuality – if we can dare to accept it there – of every part of our bodies, from eyelash to pubic hair, from nose and cheek to genitalia front and rear.

When we depersonalize our sexual identities, making them mere machineries of glandular activity, we run the risk of closing off a major form of discourse. We do not then really hear ourselves, as we perhaps have not seen ourselves. In the service of pleasure, we miss one of the greatest of pleasures – knowing ourselves as we are, speaking and understanding our own language. For sexuality is not only the body's language, it is the psyche's language too, speaking in images, affects, and fantasies that move conscious and unconscious mental processes into each other. Sexuality also speaks in its way of the spirit, expressing our longings to touch the other and achieve union. It figures often in the saints' language to describe their meetings with God.

Sexuality, in all its manifestations, brings awareness, however dim, of another toward whom the self tends. Even in its most autoerotic beginnings, instinct presses toward a release that includes a dimly apprehended state of being different, something other than our present state. Even when we are caught in autoerotic compulsions, a fantasied other or part of the other accompanies us, even if represented by a fetishistic object.

In its more mature expression, the sexual self seeks an other to enter and there make itself known, to receive and embrace. In its most happy expressions, the self in sexuality recognizes the spiritual core of the other and in that encounter finds its own. In becoming one the two become more clearly two, who together may feel themselves caught up in a larger One who holds them both in its embrace.

As we have seen in Part One (pp. 56-60), if we have known too much envy, we feel trapped in a presexual, mother-bound state. Yet we cannot take in the mother we need at the core of our own ego because we want to become her rather than ourselves. We perceive the mother as all-in-all, bisexual, creator-devourer, possessor of the male and female parts. Our egos remain weak, ill-defined, overwhelmed by the gap between us and the primordial life our mother represents – the self we are at once contained in and destined to become.

In cases of intense envy, the mother self – or anyone we envy – never gets broken into parts that we can take in one at a time: her food-giving breast, her containing belly, her holding arms, her life-producing sexual organs. Instead, she remains in her primordial undifferentiated state and remains overwhelming. Because we do not take in her parts and digest them as our own, we cannot project those body parts outward again onto the men and women around us nor become aware of archetypal images corresponding to those body parts. As a result, we cannot bring into being the contrasexual archetype which leads to the soul image of the adult person.

The mother archetype stays undifferentiated in us and becomes a force conducive to envy in us. We look at others and see in them a fulfillment we never had, a nurtured identity. Overwhelmed by our mountainous mothering, we look to steal that small, precious individuality we see in someone else. When the mother comes to us in a form and size that our own initial smallness can take in, we are made aware of ourselves, we find some of the dimensions of contentment, and are prepared to accept other selves outside of us as male or female beings in an acceptable scale of being. We have gathered in the best way possible, from an archetypal source, the sense – the image of the other.

On a personal level, when these images of the opposite sex are coherent, they animate our most important meanings with the opposite sex, expressing imaginatively what those meanings mean to us, whether negative or positive. Negatively, a woman's bruising encounter with a man can express itself in accompanying images which register that she feels not only singed by the man, but burned-out in her femininity as well. Failed love affairs or broken marriages really do have the power to crush us and lead us to avenging violence. For example, a man, utterly rejected by a woman he had lived with closely and happily, felt all but unable to get over it. It was as if the earth herself had folded her skirts against him. He despaired of ever being able to love again and was beset by violent rages toward women in general as a deceiving sex.

A happy love between a man and a woman makes each feel possible – able to risk, wanting to develop, glad about the bodies they have. Accompanying images range from feeling as if one had "come home" to be blessed by God to feeling summoned by a long-feared but desired destiny. One is made magnanimous, open to the whole world, by a steady flow of love.

But too much envy interferes with the processes that issue in adult sexual identity. The natural ordering of the self is interrupted and its parts dispersed into fragments rather than collected and unified into an integrated whole.

Envy's fragmentation of our sexual identities can take many forms. Images and body parts do not go together but war instead. A pleasurable sexual sensation, for example, becomes associated with images of degradation so that the sexual experience must be fought rather than enjoyed. One woman, for example, felt orgasm as an acutely painful "flying apart into pieces," to be avoided at all costs. A natural body thrust may seem a form of sadistic savagery, so that the only safety from such violent impulses lies in impotence. The body parts themselves, made for complementarily, instead vie and compete enviously with one another. Men envy women their breasts and vaginas and defend against the envy by denigrating the female parts as nothing but undifferentiated flesh. Their female flesh achieves distinction only by sheer irrepressible size, as in Jayne Mansfield, Anita Ekberg, or the centerfold classics. In the crucial details, it is without any individual mark: "All cats are good in the dark"; "Cover up the face and who can tell?" Women envy men their phallic organs seeing them as emblems of the male possessing all the power and mobility. They defend against envy by seeing men as only little boys or empty macho types devoid of heart or soul. They reduce men to mere flesh just as men have reduced them. And in the reduction, they utterly fail to acknowledge and hold onto their own phallicism, which is both in the flesh and in the spirit at least as much a defining part of feminine identity as it is of masculine. Each sex wants to grab the parts of the other to avoid claiming its own parts.

Envy makes war within the confines of one's own sex, too. Women envy each other, vying for first place in areas of beauty, job accomplishment, and femininity, looking always for more power. Men succumb to primitive rites of envy – testing to see who has the biggest penis, or its surrogates in bank balance, possessions, intellect, or social muscle.

Often the parts of self we cannot accept we deposit on the other sex, to be controlled and despised there, thus assuring prejudice and discrimination. Women who are trying to put together their male and female parts are criticized as mannish and coarse. Men who seek to join their female and male parts are ridiculed as effeminate and weak. Or, to avoid the dreaded and envied other, each sex tries to be both sexes in one, possessor of both sexes' organs and imagery – leading to bisexual fantasies of narcissistic omnipotence, where one is complete, needs no other, and has at last replaced mother.

If our envy is not too great, it can act as an agent of sexual and spiritual growth. Penis envy, for example, may be the initial recognition by a woman of a body part that is quite different from her own, her first attraction to bodily otherness and the world of sexual identity. The part can lead her to the whole other person, the one to whom the penis belongs. One of the ways we first learn and relate to others is by seeing one part of them at a time, only gradually adding the parts together to make up whole persons. Penis envy is perceiving a body part and what it symbolizes of another with excitement, recognizing that something good resides there. A little girl admires the long arc of urine her brother can so deftly aim; grown-up women feel grateful for the pleasure the penis brings them and also appreciate and envy its special conveniences, say, on a picnic with poison ivy around.

Envy between the sexes begins as an admiring sighting of something good. In its initial and milder forms, such envy is a step on the way to object love – to relating to the whole person who owns these interesting parts, so different from our own. An adolescent boy, for example, confided to his best friend his awe on first touching a girl's genitals, using a homely image to capture her exciting otherness: "It was like the inside of a dog's mouth." Only if envy grows too strong does the admiration sour, making us want to steal the part or use it in place of our own.

Not only can envy act as a first step toward loving a whole person of the opposite sex, it can also lead us to embrace our own particular sexuality more fully and to open our imagination to spiritual life. For the part that so attracts us, in its differences conjures up fresh images. We are led to examine what we concretely possess in contrast to what we can possess only imaginatively. The envied object exists as an archetypal symbol, not as a real part of ourselves, so it always pulls us beyond ourselves toward the other it represents. And envy may really be our first recognition of the desirability of that other – whether it is an infant looking at a mother's breast, an adult of one sex contemplating an adult of the other sex, or a soul moving toward God.

Two things follow this recognition of sexual otherness. First, what may have begun as rejection of self – wanting the other sex's parts in place of our own – may end up as self-inspection and deep acceptance of ourselves in body and spirit. We learn how our body works, the sexual pleasure it can give and receive, the imaginative life it arouses and develops. Secondly, we sense the difference between concrete physical possession and imaginative relation to something, for we can never concretely possess the penis if we are female, nor the vagina and breasts if we are male.

Only through imagination – that middle realm of images and emotions which exists between self and other – can we relate to the symbolic reality of the envied object. That is the object that introduces us to the world of spirit we share with others, where we do not possess an object but must share its existence between us. The envied object introduces us to an inner world where a man may reach over more deeply into his imaginative hold on secret nurturing spaces and a woman can penetrate ever more deeply into her sense of the phallic fount spewing forth seeds of potential life. But we do not own these objects of otherness; they are not our possessions. We can only relate to them. In this way our sexual parts and images introduce us to our spiritual parts and possibilities. We learn that the same problems that beset us sexually may also attack us spiritually. Just as when our envy grows too strong we want to steal each other's parts, so spiritually we want to possess our inner world, not relate to it, and thus to possess the good and control it.

Envy gone awry arrests our spiritual life by splitting up the symbolic parts associated with our sexuality. Human imagination has often enlisted sexual images to describe those elemental parts of being, the sky and earth, as the male and female genitals, lingam and yoni, like Cinderella's foot and its slipper. The ground that gives rise to the Word and the Word that articulates the encompassing ground are exactly parallel, as are all masculine and feminine elements. When envy grows too strong in us, we lose its signifying capacity and suffer its effects to stop us in our tracks.

All these elements stay unsorted, unseparated, undifferentiated, and confused. They are overwhelming to human perception, and inevitably falsified. Spiritually, we may construct an idealized God, whose distant perfection persecutes us with judgments of our own sin, or tantalizes us with an unreachable goodness. We often cannot get even a purchase on any notion of God. It all remains blurred, fused together, inaccessible to us. God becomes equated with psychic force or the unconscious or some useless abstraction of presence.

10

The Plight of the Good

The effects of envy on the self extend to the good itself. In the Judeo-Christian tradition, good is conceived as coming from God, the highest good, offered in Christ to those who would receive and "not take offense" in it. Envy shuts us up against the positive things we long for and makes us take deep offense in them. Envy makes us abandon the good. Our reaction does not, fortunately, succeed in destroying everything good for us, but it does cast our relation to goodness in negative terms. Thus the progression from ourself to the other who possesses something admirable still occurs, but now all its motion is negative. We move from envy of another's positive quality of being to envy of the good itself, from hunger for the good to desire to possess it, or to make it appear less desirable. Failing in those efforts, we come in our dread of everything good to attack it outright, trying to kill it. The plight of the good and the positive – the pure in heart – in the face of envy is endless suffering and sorrow.

The good are more exposed than other people because they are more receptive to the fullness of being, their own and the world's. "For the pure in heart," as Louis Lavelle says, "the world has no murky depths; they penetrate through to the well-spring of life. It may happen that they unblushingly show what others more customarily hide." There are no pretenses with such goodness, no false parts, no distorting cosmetics. "A pure soul is at all times everything that she is. Purity is the quality of the child who freely shows us his inner self, before the process of repression and distortion has set in." And so Cinderella sits in her ashes, utterly undefended except by her good heart.

She will be hurt. She must be hurt. We all must be, good or bad, pure or impure in heart. The advantage of an unenvious goodness is that no matter how savagely treated by the world around it, it does not easily become brutalized, does not join its torturers, either in reprisal or in conquest. The greatest strength of goodness, even a trampled and weeping one, is as Lavelle defines the attitude of purity, to be "a living transparency.... When we see reality in a pure enough light, we see it coming to be." And so "Purity is willing that things should be what they are."[70] It is not a smirky untroubled sweetness, but a tough-minded acceptance of being. Through such goodness we see things as they are and recognize as against its radiance the identifying marks of sin.

When we look at envy as sin, we must see our own act of will against the good. First we refuse the good. Spying the good in someone and wrongly concluding that we have no access to it, we turn away from it, denying its presence, its being, its actual goodness. We distort our own being as well. We reduce and denigrate our desire for it into mere illusory wishing, a kind of fake activity that obscures our true lack. We deny any ontological basis for our desire, refuse to see that it is rooted in and expressive of our being and capable then of bringing alive in us what we envy in another. We reduce ourselves to what we fail to possess, turning away from what is really alive in us. All we can see are the images of our desire. We are what we are not. We are all envy. We refuse to pay ourselves serious attention except in those troublesome images of what we do not have. And those we can only scorn, as the ugly sisters deride Cinderella as Christ is mocked as king of the Jews. Such scorn splits away from our consciousness the unconscious energy that urges us on to new possibilities of being. We diminish ourselves. We are diminished.

We shrink our freedom by refusing to grow up to it. We mock ourselves, in envy, rejecting the possibility of becoming our own self, whatever that may be. We shut ourselves off into what Kierkegaard calls "unfreedom," preferring muteness to self-expression, a vacuum to the fullness of our own experience, sudden eruptions to a more steady growing. What would express itself in freedom, now turns, as Kierkegaard says, into dread. What we dread is the good itself.[71]

Dante's image of the suffering of the envious frightens even the most stubborn of us. There in purgatory the envious circle eternally the edge of a cliff, each with his head on the shoulder of the next, blindly yearning for the light: "An iron thread pierces their lids and sews them up, as is done to a savage hawk who will not be quieted ... through the sutured lids, dread strains their tears leaving their cheeks all wet."[72] And all because, as one spirit confesses, he was greeting with far more pleasure another's suffering than his own successes. Thus in envy do we exclude the good as a living presence, expressive of being in another or in ourselves, or even as an objective fact.

Banished from our presence, the good appears to us as our persecutor and we do come to dread it. When something good occurs we fully expect a catastrophe to follow. Patients in analysis describe this fear dramatically. One woman says: "I panic when something good happens to me. An instant of enjoyment is followed by a voice saying, 'Don't you dare!' I'm complimented on a report sent to the president, and suddenly I fear I made a serious error and will be thrown in jail." Another woman explains that she experienced a severely restricting childhood illness as punishment for feeling "so on top of the world and successful" when she began high school. A man says bluntly: "It's dangerous to enjoy life because it will be taken away. At any moment life could be ruined." He creates intense objects of anxiety to carry his dread. If one problem gets solved, another rises to replace it.

Such dread of the good can change into active attack on anything good, as if removing its possibility entirely would relieve our anxiety. A melodrama begins to be enacted. The attack grows, moves against those around us. Innocent bystanders are suddenly imperiled, as is all too graphically depicted for us in Scripture, in Herod's murder of innocent babies in his attempt to rid himself of the threat of the infant Jesus. The drama is underlined in the liturgy by the placing of Rachel's inconsolable weeping only three days after the sweet scenes of Mary's loving welcome of the Christ-child at her breast. A maddened envy kills not only the good but anyone or anything in its vicinity. That is why Herod's slaughter of the innocents is sometimes interpreted as marking Jesus' loss of innocence, turning it to sorrow. In more ordinary life we see parents' envy constrict the talent of their children, making their children feel their gifts are not their own but only there for someone else's use. Envy sabotages our aims to develop our own skills by erecting strong barriers that new images cannot break through. Envy leads to character assassination, to rape, to murder. It encourages gossip and subtle but persistent withholding of any affirmation of another's self. Envy undermines the ground on which we stand. A few envious persons in a small community can destroy the whole, fraying connections, leaving holes through which only too many can fall.

The depredations of envy reach their climax in the organized resentment the envious show at any manifestation of the good. Jesus' words "Blessed are they who do not take offense at me" are an adroit way of speaking of the danger of such resentment of the good, such determination to wound it, if not altogether destroy it. The gospel message itself came to be described as an offense – a scandalous set of doctrines that must in themselves result in sin. In this spiritual state crucifixion becomes a plausible treatment for the offending ideas.

The reaction to those ideas takes several forms. The first is what Kierkegaard calls "unhappy admiration." As admiration-turned-envy operates between persons, so adoration-turned-offense operates between us and God: "An admirer who feels that he cannot be happy by surrendering himself elects to become envious of that which he admires. So he speaks another language, ... the thing which he really admires is called a stupid, insipid and queer sort of thing. Admiration is happy self-surrender; envy is unhappy self-assertion."[73]

Cinderella surrenders herself to gain herself. In her transparency to being she fully accepts reality. Is reality, then, so easily acceptable? Yes, if one lives so firmly, so completely in one's being. No, if one insists upon submitting the terms of one's being to reasonable analysis. What Cinderella accepts – what goodness, what innocence, what purity of heart accepts – is the absurd. She is at once Kierkegaard's Knight of Faith, that is the scriptural Abraham, and the young girl who, "in spite of all difficulties ... remains convinced that her wish will surely be fulfilled." It is not faith or her catechetical instruction that has given her such conviction, but the childish kind of innocence that has made her a wonder-worker "able to conjure the finite powers of existence and make the very stones weep."

Even Kierkegaard cannot quite go all the way with the young girl. He cannot see in her conviction a willingness to face the impossible. He does not find in her that sufficiency of resignation which must underlie faith. And yet, and yet, in a conjuring feat of his own imagination, where the absurd reigns supreme, he creates a "young swain" who falls in love with a princess well above his station. The "whole content of his life consists in this love, and yet the situation is such that it is impossible for it to be realized, impossible for it to be translated from ideality into reality." But what if the princess is "like-minded"? Then "the beautiful consequence will be apparent. She will introduce herself into that order of knighthood into which one is not received by balloting, but of which everyone is a member who has the courage to introduce himself, that order of knighthood which proves its immortality by the fact that it makes no distinction between man and woman."[74]

Kierkegaard understood the marvel of such a meeting between a man and a woman, between the young swain who is in all men and the princess who is in all women. He understood the fairy-tale dimensions of the life of faith that triumphs over resignation, the life in which, as the Russian philosopher Lev Shestov never tired of repeating, all things are possible. For Kierkegaard had missed his young-swain opportunity, had lost his princess, breaking with the young girl to whom he was engaged, Regine Olsen, running away to Berlin only on his return to find her engaged to someone else. He thought he could face the loss: "By my own strength I am able to give up the princess, and I shall not become a grumbler," he says in *Fear and Trembling*, "but shall find joy and repose in my pain." But he cannot get her back by his own strength, for he needs all of that in order to be resigned. He needs something more: "By faith I shall get her in virtue of the absurd." He needs that kind of faith, but he does not find it.

It takes a greater strength than that of resignation to grasp the absurd, not only to say, as Kierkegaard does, "And yet it must be glorious to get the princess," but to act on that prayer of hope. Shestov wonders about the man who could say, "If only I had had faith, Regine would still be mine." The questions are clear enough:

> Why is a man who strives so passionately, so frantically for faith unable to attain it? Why can he not follow the example of Abraham and the poor youth who fell in love with the king's daughter? Why has he become so heavy and incapable of soaring? Why has resignation befallen him, why has he been denied this final act of daring? [75]

The answers are not so clear and not so pleasant. It is easy enough to say, as a kind of paraphrase of Kierkegaard's whole body of work, that he could not find in himself "the capacity for the final act of daring." It was not that he could not manage the "feat of self-renunciation." It was certainly not that he lacked the reasoning power to see what was wrong and what was needed. It would have been better, in fact, if he had renounced renunciation and much better if he had, at least for a while, lost his reason.

"Humiliez-vous, raison impuissante," Pascal cries. "Humble yourself, impotent reason; be silent, foolish nature. Learn that man is infinitely beyond the understanding of man and hear from your master your true condition, of which you are ignorant."[76] The paradoxical command is shattering, even to a noble soul such as Kierkegaard. One must become a suffering servant sitting in the ashes of the hearth, not as a feat of resignation that will lead to heaven, but as a prelude to the happiness of earth. The promises of eternity do not require us to forswear the world, but on the contrary ask us to make good use of it. Even the saints must not be envied or emulated here. Even their most daring deeds must not be coveted to replace our own little timid acts and to make us into mirrors of their majesty. Their daring is theirs, not ours. Their renunciation, if that is the mark of their holiness, is for them, not for us. It may require more of us to accept our princes and princesses than to renounce them. Our great daring may well be the daring of love, which, when accepted simply, innocently, with open avowal, in our cynical age proves to be the greatest of scandals. "Why, that happens only in fairy tales!" And somebody adds, "And sometimes still in movies." Which accounts for the high readership of fairy tales and the faithful journeying of millions to view anything on the screen that may offer the prospect of a happy-ever-after ending, even homely little science-fiction sagas in which the joyous delivery is left to the plastic fingers of an extraterrestrial visitor.

We each must call on creation and the Creator in our own fashion, and the fashions are infinite as they must be when they come not from science fiction but from an infinite imagination. Some of them are more allegorical of the infinite possibilities of the finite than others. That is why, as we look for our own way of reaching eternity, or even just contemplate the idea, we respond with such a rush of libidinal energy to both a Cinderella and a Job. Each is ultimately well looked after. Each offers hope at the end of a long pilgrimage of suffering. Both strain the limits of our faith. Neither is easy to dismiss.

Fairy godmothers are harder and harder to come by. So are beneficent gods. This is the century, as a very loud and practiced chorus never tires of reminding us, of senseless carnage in Vietnam and the Middle East, of Auschwitz and the Gulag Archipelago, of an apparently endless spiral of terrorism, and we need to be reminded of these facts, if not necessarily in such accusatory tones. But it is also the time of the Cinderellas of cerebral palsy and the Jobs of retardation, who have found their fairy godmothers and beneficent gods. We have begun to reclaim our castoffs. We are beginning to match senseless acts of destruction with sensible ones of construction. The statistics may not yet provide matching columns, but the figures of rescues attempted and rescues brought off are impressive. And if it is true that we are all undone by one wanton killing, that after the death of one child in a fire raid the numbers that follow are not important, isn't it equally true that we are all re-created by the rescue of one infant from an ash heap, the extrication of one life from the terrors of autistic silence?

What Cinderella seen this way offers to our contemplation is the spectacle of a cheerful Job. She does not shake her fist at heaven. She does not need to see how pitiful her efforts are when compared to the maker of behemoths and leviathans. But, as with the blameless and upright man of Uz, her trials make her, finally, our intercessor. Taunted by her sisters as Job was by his friends, as we all are by those who demand in effect that we envy those without boils or rags or a nagging family, Cinderella shows a stubbornness like Job's. She insists on her own dreams. She surrenders to the daring of the possible. She looks, without resignation or renunciation, to the saving relationship.

When we envy we cannot surrender to the extraordinary relationship God offers. Kierkegaard describes the situation as that of an emperor suddenly noticing the existence of a day laborer, and more, actively seeking out such a person for a close relationship. Why me? the laborer wonders. To make a fool of me? So that I will become the laughingstock of the whole town, ridiculed in the newspaper, the butt of jokes and songs?[77] God's seeking us across the infinite gap between Creator and creature puts this same kind of question to us. Can we accept that God sees us and wants a connection so close to us that we can intimately reach the divine at any time?

In the grip of envy, we choose offense instead of surrender. God's offer is too good and too high for us. It makes us feel too low, too bad. Too great a distance must be traversed. The gap between us and the holy seems too great.[78] Resentfully, we reason that either God should remove the gap and be like us – not holy, not divine – or make no mention of crossing it. We focus on how lowly this makes us feel instead of on how high God promises to raise us.

Pascal and Kierkegaard see the lowest form our offense takes as our having no opinion one way or the other about what God offers. We may feel curious but remain uninvolved. This neutral spiritual state, held in such contempt in the Book of Revelation, shows us timid about closeness, to others and even to ourselves, fearful such dependency will arouse envy. We avoid envy by maintaining distance between ourselves and good objects.[79]

The middle form of offense becomes negative. We cannot let the issue go, but neither can we join it. Constantly preoccupied with God's offer, we hold it at arm's length in envious looking, never taking gladly what is offered. We lose that child's delight in presents, opening soft wrappings, spying, say, a teddy bear to take into one's arms, to rub noses with, feeling the fuzz and fingering the paws: "A bear!" A glad face and an open heart welcome the gift. But we look sourly, suspiciously, at what is offered, and question whether the wrappings are appropriate. We ask: "Is it really a bear? How do I know for certain? What evidence is there? Can it be for us, not someone else?" Or we demur, saying: "I couldn't possibly accept such a gift. It is too much. Oh, no, not for me. But thank you anyway." And then we burn with resentment if we are taken up on our refusal.

But we are almost always taken up on our refusal. How long, after all, can people stay with us and try to persuade us to accept their acts of love or goodness or simple neighborliness? How long can we put up with our own refusal of the gifts given us, the gifts that define and identify us? If we cannot be persuaded by others because of our neutrality of being, how can we persuade ourselves? Most often, if we have bogged down in that terrible middle ground of trimmerdom, where nothing is either bad enough to be totally eschewed or good enough to be eagerly accepted, we settle for a half life. We know that somehow we will be sustained in our day-to-day living by that primordial force – whatever our own name for it – Georg Groddeck called it the It, *das Es,* and Freud's translators renamed it in Latin the *Id.* That hypothetical but not unreal It lives our life, then, for us.

The effect is an extraordinary diminution of consciousness. We keep missing the vitality of being that springs up in us in almost every part, the vitality of parts that make many in the Hindu tradition uneasy about locating intelligence or the thinking process in the brain or any other sector of the body, recognizing, as they do, that understanding may suddenly come to us out of the flexing of a kneecap, the movement of a gland, or a muscle, or a nerve. We fail, then, to see and understand, as Groddeck does, that the hand, for example, has its own I and "knows what it does, and knows that it knows."

For Groddeck, the ego is the "general-I," one among untold numbers of I's in the human, for "every single separate cell has this consciousness of individuality, every tissue, every organic system." This, he admits, he cannot prove, but he insists that he must believe this as a doctor, when he sees "how the stomach can respond to certain amounts of nourishment, how it makes careful use of its secretion according to the nature and the quantity of the material applied to it, how it uses eyes, nose and mouth, as its own organs in selecting what it will enjoy." Watching all this fullness of being called forth, summoned by the unconscious that lives alongside consciousness, Groddeck says, with Cinderella-like innocence: "I have realized how beautiful life is. And every day it grows more so."[80] This, if we are sunk in the middle-ground neutrality of trimmerdom, is what we refuse. This, caught in the shuttling back and forth between acceptance and rejection that envy has made our life process, is what we repudiate – life itself.

We can go further. We can add to our turning down of life a resounding impiety in which we reject any source for life. We can join with those who declare Christianity a lie, who answer God's offer not only of life, but of a sense of what it means, with flat rejection.[81] They are those who seek instead to put to death every good thing that is offered them. They shut up against the light. Such refusers of the good are, in Pascal's strong words, those who "live without either knowing or seeking" God and who "judge themselves so little worthy of their own care that they do not deserve that others should care for them; and we need all the charity of the religion they scorn to prevent ourselves from despising them even to the point of abandoning them to their own folly."[82]

The pictures we have of Christ's varied reactions to those who have rejected him reveal the deeper dimensions of the envied ones' responses to being envied. Jesus is reported to be angry and to counsel his disciples to quit towns that do not receive them, not to waste time or energy dealing with the neutered. He tells us stories about himself going out to the doubter to let him touch his risen presence in order finally to believe. And Jesus also outlines in grim parables the fate awaiting those who refuse to use what they are given, who hide it away instead. They will find themselves cast into outer darkness, even as they turned away from the light. But then, after all this, it is Jesus who hangs on the cross, himself the victim of envy at its most lethal, and it is Jesus who submits, not answering, not defending, not retaliating, but simply holding to the good of God's design, even unto death.

11

Repentance

Goodness, finally, comprises the only solace for envy, that same goodness which aroused envy in the first place. Dostoevsky's Grand Inquisitor feels his lips burning with Christ's kiss, his only answer to the Inquisitor's passionate rejection of what the Messiah has offered humanity. But after the kiss he feels he must let Jesus go, even though he had planned to kill him. Kierkegaard says only the good in its silent presence can compel the trimmer, the shut-up neutered person, to speak. How then does goodness bring solace to our envious heart? How does it save us from the sin of envy? By sheer presence. The presence of goodness effects a fundamental change in us, moving us toward repentance, consent and correspondence to its grace.

Repentance is always painful, for it means an embarrassing about-face. We must turn around and look at the same thing from a different point of view, one we could not have even thought or imagined before. Repentance brings with it shock, as we look hard, with new eyes, at the old thing. Envy, which we felt before as a corroding emotion scarring the surface of our self-esteem as it ate into any good feeling we might have for the other, now appears as a herald of the good. Whether the envy comes from us or toward us, it is a signal now of recognizing goodness, even if negative. We enter through the back door into the presence of the good. We smell it, sense it over there. We feel alerted to its presence, as animals sensing a stranger in the dark. We wish at all costs to avoid envy. We learn to analyze it, to reduce its effects. We welcome envy now as a pointer to the good. That is a turning around!

This new set of perceptions clearly illustrates the conjunction of the spiritual and the psychological. For, finally, we must accept what comes to us in our spiritual life, what is really there in us, and confess it, if only to ourselves. Psychological analysis of the roots and effects of envy helps enormously in this hard task, but it rarely can accomplish or complete it by itself. Deep analysis can open to us the dark secret life of envy, the way it betrays us in our despair, where we see ourselves as worthless and unwanted. But such clarity does not bring healing. The healing comes from a radical change of place, which psychoanalytical insight surely encourages. But the actual changing of our place issues only from our spiritual center. With a gasp, we change our stance, find our departure point radically altered, though we are never really clear about how we got from there to here.

This is the mystery of repentance. We pray for it, knowing that repentance is a gift. We do not make it by ourselves; we are shocked by it and speak of its "before" and "after" qualities. We feel rescued by it; we know why it must be called a grace.

Repentance has a familiar and alien texture. We feel established in a new place in relation to whatever we repent. We see our envy with new eyes. Whereas, before envy separated us from the good, we see now that it brought us to it. Envy pointed to the goodness there, somewhere in the person we envied or, miraculously, here, present in ourselves. We do not focus now on who has the good but on the fact that it exists. Envy becomes a doorway to the good. How very far from its old ways! The sin of taking offense at the good has been transformed into the sin that opens to the grace of seeing the good.

We reach this way to the primordial source of faith in being which some of us see as antecedent to everything else in human yearning. We are striving somehow, in the shock of repentance, to appease the hunger for self which is at the beginning of everything for us, looking for even the wispiest sense of our own self. The enlarged image of himself that we grow toward, as the philosopher R. G. Collingwood stresses, is our first perception of God. It is a more important understanding of God than fear provides and probably comes first. We cannot really do more than grope toward it when we are still deeply possessed by envy, but as repentance mounts and grace falls on us we recognize that a lovable otherness exists not only in God but in us ourselves. We see the possibility of overcoming the loneliness which envy enforces and which has until now been so enervating in our lives. We begin to gather strength. "Loneliness is a kind of weakness," as Collingwood says, "and attachment is a kind of strength; but a special kind. Strength as such, the strength that a hungry man wants, is his own strength, the strength of a self *which he is.* This new kind of strength is a strength he borrows from something else, the strength of *something he has.*" The "something," the "other thing," Collingwood calls our "second self."[83]

It is a marvelous beginning we make here because it has such an intriguing movement, doubling back on itself, moving down to move up, moving up to move in. We are called out of self, in envious preoccupation with the achievement and success and appeal of others, in order to be called back into self as we recognize in our second self the strength which we possess, the strength which we are. There we may find, at least in the most rudimentary terms, the God who gave us our strength.

But this is only a beginning and it has its dangers. We may find ourselves so caught up in the newly discovered strength that we have room for nothing else. "Look," we keep saying to ourselves, like Scrooge discovering Christmas, "look at the good in me! See what I am, see what I can do!" And we can do a great deal and it is good. But it is not yet all there, all in place. Envy, which springs from an emptiness of being, has made us lonely, weak, and slothful about our own gifts. Now, we have a way of filling the loneliness, of acquiring force and energy. But they will remain mere abstractions to us and lead to an even greater loneliness and despondency if we do not stop to reflect on the whole astonishing process in which we have been caught up. We must accept as part of our reality the envy that so gripped us until now and narrowed our lives, just as we take in the possibility of escape from envy and the expansion of our lives that will bring with it. Envy remains near to us, but positively near now, where in the past it was negatively near. It is a movement within us now that, properly nurtured, may bring more strength and an even greater enlargement of self.

The nearness of envy comes in many new ways. Cinderella and her sisters are two parts of one envy complex. As we said in Part One (pp. 77-79), each of them must recognize the opposite emotion within her. The envied one must open to the possibility of envying, and the envier to the possibility of being envied, for each emotion circulates around the same presence of the good and dread of it. Each one, looking at the good from an unaccustomed point of view, must reach to the whole conflict within herself, no longer parceling out half of it onto the other.

For each of us, it may be a little different, but we all must come to terms with some unclaimed emotion around envy. Some of us who are envied do not respond with envy, but know, sadly, the emptiness and loss of self-esteem envy inflicts. In order to avoid envious attack, we may disavow our own good self. For example, a woman recalls recurrent childhood experiences of feeling happy and alive about something and having others attack her, saying: "Oh, you just think you're so great!" She would think, "I shouldn't be so happy, when really I'm no good at all." And then she would let go of the good things she felt happy about. Although such a reaction makes sense, we must see how wrong it is to let go of any part of the good. It is our own act, not just a reaction to something done to us. We are ourselves responsible, no matter how greatly provoked. Even if our parents, for example, did not stand by our real self, and thereby established a bad procedure that we introjected and imitated, we must also see where we ourselves deserted our true self and abandoned it out of fear of envy and thereby contributed to our inner emptiness.

It is both a practical matter to recognize our desertion of self and a philosophical one. We have no chance of reclaiming our abandoned selves if we do not admit that, in the final reckoning, *we* left them out, *we* let them go, no one else. We have every chance of admitting what must be admitted when we see that what we have been dealing with is evil and that it is evil's special quality to appear to be and not to be at the same time. This is its defining mystery. The only way of facing it is, as Gabriel Marcel points out in a handsome refurbishing of a Kierkegaardian paradox: "Evil is real. We cannot deny its reality without diminishing the basic seriousness of existence and thus falling into a kind of nonsense, a dreadful buffoonery. And yet evil is not real absolutely speaking." Evil, he is saying, as so many since Augustine have said, is the privation of being, and yet it is very much with us, more alive in its denials than many other things in their affirmations. What do we do, then, with this acknowledged evil? We turn from it, not, as Marcel suggests, with "certitude, but rather a faith in the possibility of overcoming it – not abstractly, of course, by adhering to a theory or theodicy, but *hic et nunc*" – here and now, in the immediacy of our emptiness.

It is a privileged process, for it confirms the positive element in that negativity which must at some time or another afflict all of us. It is what sustains us, if we are daring enough to think about all we can do in the light of what we have not done. "And what would we be," Marcel asks, "and what would the difficult journeying which is our very way of existing be, without the light, which is so easy both to see and to miss, and which lights every man who comes into the world?"[84]

Envy, then, is a movement into the light. Its darkness is a means of revelation, which does not mean that we should bless it – if by that we mean how glad we are that it exists. But, in another sense, of course we must bless it, for it does both exist and not exist in the terrible paradoxical way of evil, and we must give thanks as we claim the gathering of feeling in us around envy, as we make room for the goodness which is a presence of being to replace the absence of being which is evil.

As envied ones we must accept the violent negative reactions stirred up by the intrusion of another's envy as revealing something about our own character. Many of us, when envied, want to retaliate, feeling hate, wishing to hurt the other as we have been hurt. We have a desire to push everything away, which can extend even to repudiating the good in ourselves that occasioned another's envy. But we must claim our hate as our own, not entirely created by others even if elicited by them. It is something arising from ourselves that we must consciously acknowledge and assume as our responsibility. Such conscious acceptance of our own pushing away from the good comprises the concreteness of our confession.

When we accept what we have done, and fully acknowledge our negative feelings for the envier, we can connect to the envier, who bursts with similar emotional experiences. We can forge a link to something opposite to us that had before remained unknown to us. We now know in ourselves some of the torments envy can stir up. To confess this knowledge means to carry it as our burden, no longer to experience it as a neighbor's burden thrust on us. Now we willingly take it up and share in its carrying.

To repent such attitudes means to own them and recognize that we have been only too willing ourselves to discard that troublesome goodness which attracts envy and embroils us in our own kind of hatred in response. The repentance introduces a radical change in us. Where there was only conscious dread of the good, there now is a warm expectation of it. No longer is the goodness just a happy possession which might bring pleasure to the one who owns it. Almost any good quality takes on a presence before us that is fearful and wonderful. We see that goodness constellates evil, that it sheds enough light for us to see the darkness. The envied one totally experiences – and admits to – the temptation to refuse the good in order to avoid the onslaught of evil it brings with it. We lose our innocence.

Similarly, when we envy we must reach to the opposite side, connecting to the good that arouses such envy. Whether it is in us or the other, the good is there and must be accepted and wherever possible admired. Instead of sinking down into despondency at our lack of what another possesses in such abundance, we must reach toward that plenty with all the wonder and pleasure it can arouse.

The humpbacked little girl Sichel in Elisabeth Langgässer's brilliant novel *The Quest*, which allegorizes the effects of Nazism on the Germans, feels great pleasure confronting her beautiful little friend Florentine in a lovely pale-blue tafetta dress. Sichel is carried away by Florentine's beauty rather than being caught in her own ugliness: "... the very essence of beauty, beauty itself: this it was that buried its talons in me." In the novel, Sichel is looking back and describing how, as a child, beauty struck her and took her into God. She had been staring with rapt attention at a milk-white stone. Its extraordinary color and smoothness hit her with the "violence of a revelation, a pure, direct vision of absolute beauty." The stone has become her special secret possession, which she hides away in her woolen mitten. Caught up in its "quiet radiance," she

> slips into that long-forgotten, magical rhythm that brings her into harmony with existence, which, though she cannot know it, is the rhythm of the spheres.... What a childhood! Drawn into the primal state of existence, she experiences in the doll the mandragora, in the top the rings of Saturn and in the crystal marble the depths of the world reduced to its essence ... [she] enters effortlessly into the pleasure of perfect freedom.[85]

For the envier, repentance consists in accepting as fact that goodness really does turn toward us, in the flesh, in others, and that we cannot shirk its presence by complaining it exists in others rather than in ourselves. Our envy is revealed as a defense against the good, a whining about where it is or is not to avoid dealing with it at all.

Though we are always on the lookout for instant revelation, the kind on which advertising, television, and false prophets thrive, we do not have much patience with the slow variety, of the sort that reveals envy as a defense against the good. For almost a century, we have had at our disposal Nietzsche's brilliant analysis of what he calls "master-morality" and "slave-morality" in *The Genealogy of Morals*, but we have not been willing very often to give it the slow, impartial inspection it deserves and to see how much of it applies to our own world. We have had Max Scheler's *Ressentiment* since 1915, a work that not only deepens Nietzsche's use of the French word to describe the feelings of frustration, impotence, sullen hostility, and vengeful resentment which characterize slave-morality, but corrects his smoking anger and the excesses of judgment that go with it. But Scheler, too, though respected by many philosophers and sociologists and given an extended outing in English in the years when phenomenological thought was once again arousing such interest in the 1960s and early 1970s, has not been greatly heeded in his Nietzschean thesis, for what he has to say is highly uncomfortable for many of us. He is all but contemptuous of modern humanitarian love, which for him "is by no means based on a spontaneous and original *affirmation of a positive value*, but on a *protest, a counter-impulse* (hatred, envy, revenge, etc.) against ruling minorities that are known to be in the possession of positive values." He is not impressed by the humanitarian love of "mankind," but sees it as "the expression of a repressed rejection, of a counter-impulse against God," which merely disguises "a repressed hatred of God."

Scheler is not without compassion for the victims of modern society, for they include all of us. But he insists that we – and they – recognize how much they victimize themselves. He suggests an abbreviated typology of the self-victimizing *ressentiment* phenomenon. There are women whose passivity and rejection generate vindictive resentment. There are those

old spinsters who respond to others' sexual pleasure with a
savage prudery. The old generally, who at any time may be
expected to respond to the oncoming youth with discomfort,
fall into *ressentiment* with particular ease in our time, in
which everything changes so quickly, from building styles to
political regimes. Families, filled with envy and hostility,
compete among themselves for power, as do certain kinds of
criminals. The priest is "condemned" to surface control of all
feelings and must gain his victories through "suffering rather
than combat." He also lists, but does not examine, "the
disappearing class of artisans ... the petty bourgeoisie and ...
small officials," and then concludes his typology with the
"apostate," who does not turn positively to his new convic-
tions but engages rather "in a continuous chain of acts of
revenge against his own spiritual past," and that type of
romanticism "which attributes creative power to mere *nega-
tion and criticism.*"

In each of these categories, Scheler sees the tensions that
develop when hatred and envy confront their own powerless-
ness. The ultimate effect is a fundamental reversal of values, a
"systematic perversion and reinterpretation" which proceeds
"until what was 'evil' appears to be 'good.'" The nadir of this
transvaluation of values is that empty-minded altruism which
insists we love others simply because they are other. For
Scheler, this is like the psychotic patient who "has become
incapable of feeling and experiencing anything 'by himself,'"
who, without any "center and focus" of his own, must live in
another's life and suffer from it, hurting himself only to give
pain to the other. In the same way, he sees in many of those
who are filled with the "universal love of mankind" the
displaced love of children who were not received with love,
who, for whatever reason, "felt 'out of place' at home." Rejected
by their families, they protest "through intense enthusiasm for
'mankind.'" But this is not love, it is a "repressed *hatred* of the
family and the immediate surroundings."[86]

Our name for this phenomenon is *utopian envy*. It is the
dream of replacing the whole defective human enterprise,

which at times seems to be squarely directed against oneself, with a perfect world, one in which love and goodness will be assured – by law. Until then, we will enforce the move from a bad world to a good one by removing one way or another all those whose goodness stands in our way.

Recognizing the good entails realizing that it does not summarily banish evil but rather enters even where evil is. As Lady Julian says, "God creates all good and suffers all evil." Thus repentance includes confessing that in our simplemindedness we cherished an idealized goodness that could cure all misery, heal all illness, make everyone happy and friendly, in short, rescue the world from every sorrow and injustice. We must recognize that we prefer our version of ideal good, perfect good, cure-all good, too-good-to-be-true good, to goodness itself. The envier begins to catch sight of the perspective of the envied one, and through the envied one of goodness itself. This is a sorrowing goodness that feels the attacks against itself, a suffering goodness that enters into the miseries of those caught in evil, a good-enough goodness that survives all the fear, dread, and envy unleashed against it. No longer can the envier set up goodness as a prize to be snatched, a talisman to banish all hardship. No more of "If only I had had the advantages you had, then I would have...." The good takes the hardship into itself, persisting despite the fact that it is persecuted, despised, or rejected.

Goodness continues to turn toward us as a living presence, though ambiguous, shadowed, sometimes even hidden. Seeing this, the envier can consciously recognize the temptation envy really represents against goodness, the evasions, the ploys, the elaborate dodges to avoid the good. The envier can now contemplate the possibility of just receiving the good as it is, looking at it, opening to it, feeling it and the changes it brings.

Repentance of envy has a large social dimension. Schoeck outlines the radical change Christian belief effected against the collective pressures of envy.[87] Here was a God who did not envy his creatures, as Zeus did, for example. This God loved his flock, and his wrath was aroused only when they were unfaithful to him. He was a jealous God but not an envious one. He grew angry out of love, not out of the wish to hurt or belittle. So the fear that the good might call down the vengeance of the divine lessened in Christians and allowed them to use their energies for every sort of advancement, personal, social, and technological. In pre-Christian theologies, prosperity was seen as a sign of the favor of the gods, a favor that could just as quickly be withdrawn by those gods who envied their creatures' success. Now here was a God who supported and encouraged human achievement and creativity, a loving one, not an envious one.

New Testament faith preaches an unenvying attitude among persons. God's love and grace flows to all, regardless of talent, beauty, degree of consciousness, class, education, color, race, sex – all those distinctions so easily conscripted into the machinery of envy.[88] The love is not offered abstractly, to some residual perfection existing in us. Instead, we are asked to bring ourselves, in whatever incompleteness or imperfection, with whatever amount of charm or wit or beauty we might possess, to others similarly well or poorly equipped. We are to love and be loved as individuals. Thus, in one stroke, believers are liberated from fear of envy of the gods and fear of their neighbors' envy. Instead, their belief about the unseen world backs their play in the visible world. Belief in the good as available to all and as at its best when shared sets loose a new emotional freedom and possibility of community action and development of skills, intellect, art, talents. No longer does one have to hide talent or possible insight lest a neighbor's envious eye sets loose persecution.

But, says Schoeck, even this new freedom fell victim in time to envy's perverting power. Equality of access to God's grace and love became translated into a guilt-laden duty to manufacture an egalitarian society on earth, where no one must exceed one's neighbor, or be inferior to him or her, thus reintroducing the leveling social policy where no one may be different from anyone else. The envy barrier, so prevalent in primitive society, where members of a tribe keep envious watch against any innovation, thus effectively preventing progress, was reintroduced with a vengeance into modern society. For now it is held to be the fault of the envied ones that the enviers envy them. Their envy proves that the envied have failed in their mission to make all equal on earth because, it is said, in a remarkable reading of Christian doctrine, all are equal before God and therefore must be equal in every other way, too – talent, position, recompense, standing in society.[89]

Schoeck recognizes that envy can also be used to perpetuate unjust social inequality. What he is after is camouflaged envy, pretending to be concern for injustice, which ends by holding the envied as responsible for the existence of envy in the envying. Repentance must include, then, being brought back to the true Christian position where we are liberated from fear of envy by God or by neighbor.

The profound truth that underlies this liberating force of Christianity is that simply existing side by side with our neighbors, from the human to the divine, confirms our existence and gives promise and warmth to it. At the lowest level, this means, as José Ortega y Gasset delights in pointing out, even if I "loathe" some other person, I must "frequent" the other, "since even if I should prefer that the other did not exist, because I loathe him, it turns out that I irremediably exist for him, and this obliges me, willy-nilly, to reckon with him and with his intentions toward me, which perhaps are malevolent. This mutual 'reckoning with,' *reciprocity*, is the first fact that we can classify as *social*." It is in the meetings with others, pleasant or unpleasant, that we discover that we are alive.

It gets better. We discover in the other person an "I" that is not our "I," the urgent reality that forms the basis of Husserl's *Cartesian Meditations* and produces a lively extended meditation in Ortega that ends in some sharp observations about the nature of woman as distinguished from man. He sums up: "The erotic attraction that woman produces in man is not – as the ascetics have always told us in their blindness on these matters – aroused by the feminine body as body; rather, we

desire woman because her body is a soul."[90] Whether we agree
or disagree, we surely must see here the range of understanding that comes when we take on the inequalities among us, of
sex or age or positions or gifts or limitations, and seize the
identifying marks of otherness, not as an opportunity for envy,
but as a chance for that confirmation of being which changes
fear into hope.

12

Consent

Repentance yields grace. It opens us to something new that could not be found or even imagined before. Repentance also yields consent. We say yes to the bits and pieces of being that come to us, being that turns out to be good.

One woman in analysis expressed this consent as she found a way out of writer's block: "I do not have to have the whole thing sewed up, perfect before I begin, but only have to attend to each part." An idealized, all-finished goodness yields to a good-enough goodness that comes in small parts, often mere crumbs, one bit at a time.

This is how community develops – Christian community, organic community. It is not a mere "aggregation of parts," fulfilling the laws of a mechanical biology, as Max Scheler stresses near the end of his great essay on *ressentiment*. The parts come together the way organs are formed, under the guidance of an "agent" which infuses each of the parts. We can understand the process only "if we assume that the *whole* unitary living being is active in each organ and that – in accordance with Kant's correct definition of the nature of the organism – the parts are not only there for the whole, but 'the whole for the parts.'"[91] We are not machines or tools, not any one of us, not any group of us, not all of us put together. We cannot be understood by reading blueprints or computer printouts, nor can we understand those things which are most lasting and that really matter by such means. We must look at people and the world around us, we must look at ourselves, with whatever parts we possess, with whatever parts we ourselves are – and accept them. Love, goodness, what really matters – all will come to us, part by part, as we in our parts move to take each of these central parts of being into ourselves, without fear that we will not be up to the undertaking and without shame that we must work within the limitations of our own individual nature and being.

Unlike the dreamer (in Chapter 2), captured by the large blunt fish that symbolized her mother's intrusive goodness, here goodness empties and accommodates itself to our size and ability to take it in. Goodness turns up in ordinary events as well as great moments: someone's kindness in bringing us food when we are sick; a child's enthusiasm to be of help; an unexpected courtesy when someone notices we are upset; a church taking up special collections to pay someone's hospital bills; a nun substituting herself for another prisoner in the line of victims to be gassed at Auschwitz; an elderly man repeatedly pushing other victims of a plane crash before himself into a helicopter's rescue halter until he himself sinks in icy river waters. We never know when goodness will seize us; we are often as surprised when we are on the giving end as when we receive gestures from others.

The healing comes in the great change from wholes to parts. We no longer have to grab at the whole goodness as if it were the first prize in a lottery. We can consent to bits and pieces as they move in and among ourselves. We live with parts. As in the miracle of the loaves and fishes, we are amazed at how many parts there are and how bountiful the crumbs left over, far beyond our needs. And those parts exist even among the hatred, the slightings, the avoidings, and denyings of the good. The particles persist and make their presence known, just as Cinderella's nighttime ball gown turns up to be worn between wearings of her daytime rags.

Consent means choosing to go toward the bits and pieces, to hold them, spend them, give them, take them, using the parts, wherever and whenever they turn up. Sometimes it means relinquishing the aim of becoming whole and consenting to live with this big rent in one's being, this wounded condition of our world. Consent often means giving up utopian solutions, or anything like them, in favor of short-term, realizable remedies. Consent means not losing our appetite for the good despite the suffering and savagery that continues to exist alongside it.

To consent to goodness means to stop asking the questions of disillusionment: "What good does it do?" "How will that change anything?" We object to the presence of goodness as ineffectual because it does not immediately bring about what we want. This turns up often enough in analysis. A person achieves an insight into a thorny complex, only to ask, sometimes in tears: "But what difference does that make? So now I know why I'm frightened. I'm still frightened. How does that improve the situation?" The question conceals the ego's defiance, its refusal to yield to experiencing the insight and let go of the solution. The very question betrays the fear of feeling the uncovered fear. When a fear is consented to, a patient can enter it fully and accept it as a long missing, hidden part, now there to be claimed. That is the true cause for rejoicing. What was lost has been found. That should be enough for the moment: to find it and knit it into the rest of oneself. What will come of it must remain to be seen and understood. We do not have to know everything right away, just the part that has been handed to us. Entering into that part, working with it, slowly, trying to know its shape and fit it into the larger puzzle, not just the enigma of our own personality but of others and of where it all may fit into the general scheme of our life, is to sense the whole from the inside out through the living of it, instead of trying to know the whole from the outside in, from the safe distance of the unparticipating spectator.

Consent to the good means to dissolve our resistance to it. Our willpower softens into a willingness to go with the part, and to work to piece the parts together. The good is not an object of knowledge, but part of our living subjectivity. Found by the heart that desires it, it meets that willingness and enlarges it.

Consent of this kind is not a weak-kneed complaisance or a trimmer's empty-soured acceptance of everything that is simply because it is. This is not collusion with the status quo. Its strength comes as Cinderella's does, from an interior nobility of being, which, as much as anything else, accounts for her extraordinary hold on our imagination almost as soon as our imagination is old enough to work at all. The interior nobility which motivates consent to goodness as we are using the words here resembles remarkably the exterior nobility that Georg Simmel described in his pioneering *Soziologie* of 1908.

Simmel's nobility rests upon the "self-assurance and autonomy" of a mediating class that is open and welcoming to others at both ends of the class structure, upper and lower. That openness and an accompanying wide latitude of behavior do not reflect an undisciplined permissiveness in the nobility. Nobles in Simmel's world know one another because they know themselves, and each shares easily in the achievement of others in any given group of the noble, whether of family or country or era. There is a determination, "a singular tenacity in the conservation of its 'objective spirit,' the achievement of individuals that is crystallized in tradition, rigid form, the products of labor, and so on." From the vantage point of pre-World War I Germany, at least, the nobility seemed to possess, like gold and silver, a "relative indestructibility." This reasoning was not any adherence on Simmel's part to mere institutions or bloodlines. He was talking rather about an "imperishability of value" that nobility claimed for itself, not the result of "services," of particular achievements, such as the Russians so long demanded of their nobles, producing only endless factional rivalry and violent conflict as well.

A nobility of "solid substance" is "like an island in the world. It is comparable to a work of art, within which each part also takes its meaning from the whole." The aesthetic appeal of the nobility is analogous to the work of art – the "charm ... of autonomy and insularity, of the solidarity of parts." But without "a creative power flowing out of the individual," an unmistakable weakness and decadent emptiness may settle in. The forms must not be too binding. The parts, however much they may owe to the whole, must also be discernible: "The distinguishing characteristic of the nobility is that ... personality, freedom, the internally grounded ... became of greater value and of greater significance here than in other structures." Neither group pressures nor the impulse to center everything in oneself could be allowed to dominate. "In its purest historical manifestations, the nobility pulls the worth of individual lives into its collective structure with unique power."

All the apparatus of an informed consent is constructed into the balance of parts Simmel is describing. When it works, it does not depend upon an inherited place in the aristocracy, but families certainly have much to do with it, and the values that families may or may not nurture are major determinants. We do not arise formed in our goodness, defined in ourselves, from an industrial proletariat, an agricultural class, the petite bourgeoisie, or any of the many strata that sociologists and others have been so busily building for us to fit into: lower middle, upper middle, upper upper, or whatever. We come as individuals out of much smaller groupings, with our own quite precise species of growth and formation. Sometimes, we achieve that most significant of the values Simmel attributes to a true nobility, the self-sufficiency of an individual within the totality of his environment. That "equation between the totality and the individual, between the predetermined givenness and the personal elaboration of life," is what Simmel defines as the "historically unique solution" of the nobility.[92]

Simmel's description applies still more accurately to the nobility that interiorizes itself than it does to the one that, whatever its accomplishments, must ultimately depend upon its rank in Burke's Peerage or the Almanach de Gotha. The nobility of inner consent is a classless society that has as many parts as a society of classes but that makes no invidious distinctions among them. We are neither so afraid of failure nor so frightened by success, if we belong to this nobility or even simply want to belong, that we must envy anyone his or her place in the world. We consent to all the parts: his, hers, theirs, ours.

When we consent to all the parts, a new view of goodness shows itself to us as a presence that consents to us. The New Testament text about God knowing and holding onto each hair on our heads makes this point, as do the parables about the shepherd looking for the lost sheep and the widow sweeping her house to search for the lost mite. Here are pictures of God caring about each part, searching for it, to bring it back into the whole. Each part is seen as distinct and as counting for something: the individual matters; the specific concrete person and even the bits of the person matter. What a comforting disclosure!

But it is a disclosure that surpasses comfort, for it begins to make clear that we are ourselves the parts that make up the whole. We must see that we are sought precisely as the specific part each of us is, not because we conform to someone else's conception of us, but because we are, each of us, simply who we are, each of us loved for our unique and irreplaceable self. That is the particular self Christ dies for.

And Christ does die – and all good people live and die – for each particular self. Each life, each death, is a treasured particularity, whether it is of the heroic proportions of the saints, or the touching figures of fairy tale and legend and literature who achieve high virtue, or anyone else, no matter how small in comparison. Size comes in the marks of individual identity. That is one reason why there is no final revelation. We must each of us add our insights to the vision of Scripture. The Russians with their special attachment to the doctrine of the transfiguration have great understanding here. They see us coming one at a time to be made over in the light, each according to our own lights. The most generously gifted among us "could only give his own version of that living Truth

– one of its many possible aspects," says S. L. Frank, a Russian philosopher particularly well-equipped to make clear to us what it means to have "God with us":

> In the last resort "the essence of Christianity" is accessible not to the individual, but to the collective experience of mankind; it finds expression in the testimony of Christian life and thought as a whole at its best and highest; the true mirror of it is the whole galaxy of Christian saints and sages. It is only in this all-embracing unity of the manifold that there is given us concretely and as it were stereoscopically that which the living image of Christ teaches us and contains for us – the true "essence of Christianity."[93]

And so we must see and hear "stereoscopically," with both eyes, with both ears, distinguishing every facet of the revelation that only we in our odd, precious, incomparable way can make out. We must consent not only to be but to be ourselves. That is a defense, not only against envy, but anger and pride as well, and all the other failures of being that we call sin. That is how we come with confidence into the fullness of life that is everybody's inheritance but that only those can take up who one way or another recognize that God is with them and in them. That is why those who are close to being and to the maker of being can say what is said in the prayer of consent so simply and so briefly. The poet Rainer Maria Rilke, in such a prayerful address, says *Du, Nachbar Gott*, "Thou my neighbor, God." Augustine puts it in terms that, for Frank, sum up the whole relationship of the human and the divine where we so often feel that God has deserted us but where in fact we have left God: "Thou hast always been with me but I have not always been with myself." And even more concisely: *Viderim me – viderim Te*, "If I saw myself I would see Thee."[94] That is the psychological richness of the theology of consent. When we accept willingly not only that we are but what we are, we also accept our neighbor's being, the man or woman next to us, the God who is both here and there. We have a meeting with self that includes by prayerful understanding every other self. The fearful dilemmas of philosophy that make some so uneasy about ever being able to prove that anybody else really exists, and just as uncomfortable at having to depend then upon ourselves as proof and witness of ourselves – all these and similar puzzlements disappear in the grace of consent.

13

Corresponding to Grace

Consenting moves us deeply into the mystery of the good. We see that it comes to us only in parts and that we are the parts to be put together into the order of creation which will bring that much-looked-for wholeness. Corresponding to the good – to grace – means cooperating with the parts given us, using them and seeing ourselves as being used, trying to fit them this way and that into the whole puzzle. The patient who finds her missing fear, for example, allows it to enter her and to be part of the whole of her, no longer abandoned. She houses it without reducing herself to the fear, just as Cinderella makes room for each part – the rags, the ball gown, the ashes, the fairy godmother – and is all the more herself for doing so. That way she grows toward wholeness. Fitting in one part rearranges the pattern of the whole of a woman and changes her in concrete and vital ways. No longer denying a hungry part of herself, for example, she can recognize more compassionately the hungry parts of her children, of her friends, of people in the world.

It is all a matter of parts, seeing other people's, seeing our own – and loving them. It is not an easy exercise, especially if one feels in any way empty or deprived. But it is an essential exercise, particularly directed to combat the deprivations of envy – to reach out in love when we ourselves feel unfulfilled, empty, unloved. As Augustine says in a shrewd passage on envy, "If you love, you are not one that has nothing." In the largest and the smallest sense, when we come together in any kind of unity, what I have is yours and what you have is mine. Augustine's metaphor for the kind of joining together in love that combats the separations of envy is the way of the parts of the body: "The eye alone in the body sees, but is it for itself alone that the eye sees? It sees both for the hand and the foot, and for the other members of the body. For if a blow is coming toward the foot, the eye doesn't turn itself away, refusing to give warning of danger. Again, the hand in the body works well enough, but is it only for itself? It also works for the eye. If a blow is directed, not at the hand, but at the face, does the hand say, 'I shall not stir; it's not coming at me'? And so the foot serves all the members, by walking, and the tongue speaks for all the rest of the body which is silent."[95]

The psychoanalyst Groddeck marvels over the independence of each of the parts of the body, seeing a separate consciousness in each of them from which we may learn how to understand ourselves and others. The theologian Augustine meditates on the interdependence of the parts of the body, seeing an extraordinary mutuality in them from which we may learn how to love ourselves and others. The different gifts we are given in our body teach us this. They do not amount to very much by themselves, however much we may prize a given moment's seeing or hearing or tasting or feeling or smelling. But when we bring them together, they defend us, they hold us together, they define us and permit us to see and hold and bring others together in love. That is why no part of us is too small to be seen – not the least little bit – or to be accepted.

Accepting the good bit given is the way we correspond to the good, which comes to us as grace, something that happens which we could not bring about by our efforts alone, but which intimately connects with the efforts we do make, confirming them, making them succeed. Grace does not cancel or substitute for our own efforts because it does not depend on them. The paradox of grace consists in both its making actual what we strove for but could not achieve and its coming as something very different from what we thought we wanted. Grace surprises us as always more than we expected and as coming from the most unlikely corners of our lives. While it comes entirely in its own terms, it endorses us, recognizing what we tried to do.

Envying or being envied shows the good as a commodity to be possessed and ourselves as the happy potential owner of the prize or its potential would-be robber. When we correspond to goodness, and put the parts together, we see that goodness is not an object but an inner integrity, not a predictable thing guaranteed to make us happy, but a relationship with something alive and responsive to small specific events in our lives. Goodness is not a norm or set of rules which we fall short of achieving and then blame ourselves for failing, but a radiance making perceptible the essential being of all things, no matter how trivial.

Thus goodness is neither, as we thought, a persecuting force nor an envied possession, but a presence issuing its own demands upon us. Goodness summons us to step toward our integrity in fitting together everything, the damaged parts as well as the healthy, with nothing left out. That includes the part of envy, too – whether we are the envier or the envied. Envy is forgiven, not eradicated, bound up into the whole, not annihilated, held now in a larger recognition of the good with its own oblique salute to it. Instead of taking offense, we behold the good there with us, altogether present.

In repentance, we see that goodness had turned to us before we turned to it. Our turning is a response to a prior presence. In consenting to the good, we discover goodness has consented to us. In corresponding to the graces given us we come upon a goodness very different from our imaginings.

Goodness discloses itself as the connecting link that makes a whole out of the parts, that produces a presence instead of an absence. This is a constructed wholeness, not a magic gift, not a fusion that extinguishes parts, but a bringing together of all the bits in a purposeful and tough-minded wholeness. We are summoned to our best self, and discover that that means nothing is thrown back or segregated. For example, a person caught in a pathological narcissism covers up a serious wound to the self by identifying with some parts as if they were the whole – relying on a tricky talent to hide a feeling of being unlovable, or an elaborate outer physical beauty to hide a feeling of inner ugliness. This disorder is healed when narcissistic energies can be invested in the links between these parts, the ugliness joining up with the beauty, the unlovable feeling with the talent.[96] The good really reaches to all of what is in us, offering itself to the outcast and dejected as well as to the established and strong parts. No part should take offense; each must take hold.

On a collective level, a society must make provision for envy, accepting it as an inevitable human emotion, made only the more destructive when its very existence is denied in a politics that promises an envy-free utopia. The antidote for outer-population disorders resembles the one for our inner population, and vice versa. Energy must be invested in the connections that link all the parts together, where the good is recognized as something that does not fully exist until it is shared.

The Cinderella tale gives an interesting clue to how this begins to be done by recovering the value of the feminine part. A woman must look for the feminine, find it, acknowledge it, affirm it, like Cinderella. She must join with it, raise it to equal power with the masculine, so that it governs consciously in relation to its princely mate when it becomes visible, as it does in the fairy tale. The feminine symbolizes a mode of consciousness that recognizes what is, and the value of all the little parts that exist together, rather than emphasizing what should be to the exclusion of those parts.[97]

Vasily Rozanov, that startling figure who wandered through the destruction and terror of the Russian Revolution turning out pamphlets proclaiming *The Apocalypse of Our Time*, saw a Cinderella-like young girl as the embodiment of true observation, of true consciousness in an unconscious, unseeing world. "You did not pass by the world, young girl ...

oh, the gentlest among the gentle," he wrote in one of his apocalyptic pamphlets. "You looked thoughtfully.... You observed lovingly.... You burst into song.... You were not envious." Rozanov's girl wants to join the world around her, to become a part of it. "Your heart went out to everything. And you longed to add your voice to the choir." The tragedy of this time, 1917 to 1919, is that no one notices such gentle acceptance of full consciousness: "No one noticed you, and they did not want your songs. And so there you are, standing by."

Rozanov vows to remain with his gentle girl, to stand by her side until the end of the world. In her recognition of everything around her, of what is, of being itself, he sees an anticipation of eternity. This is where justice is, with her, and with him standing by her, while the world that ignores her is "truly unjust."[98] And, we might add, the world that ignores itself is truly unjust, for what it must see and take in is everything, making room for the good beside the bad and the bad beside the good, for the envied beside the envying and the envying beside the envied.

For a society consciously to make provision for an envious part means making space for it in social process, allowing it to link up with what would soften and modify it, so that its degree may be mild enough to make envy a catalytic agent for transformation rather than a destructive terror. Envy may then become a force for the emulation of the good in a way that encourages growth and development and does not lead to guilt and persecution. For example, the simple recognition that envy arises in the envier and not in the envied would help us avoid those elaborate schemes of social engineering that promise to remove envy, but in fact only package it in different forms, and if anything, increase it. Recognizing envy's inevitable appearance in our lives may spur a society to foster attention to the realities that are the only solace and cure for envy's miseries: not war and social revolution, but the values inherent in art and religion, and the recognition of the special value of each individual, all those living parts without whom society cannot be a whole. Thus the being of each citizen must be addressed by the powers and policies of the whole society, taking measures economically and politically to secure and enrich each citizen, the basic minority, the minority of one – of a retardate or a genius, of an autistic child or a prodigy, of an athlete or a scholar or an assembly-line worker. Being before doing, value before formulas – those are the crucial attitudes. Making social provisions for envy means recognizing all our efforts as partial. They may only be parts, but without them there is no whole. Human efforts must link up with parts that cannot be manufactured or willed – those which make us touching in our folly, reachable in our awkwardness – with love and mercy and grace.

14

Goodness

Goodness displays itself as the linking of the most unlikely parts together: male and female, body and spirit, death and life. The envy between the sexes is gathered into the figure of Christ who, as male, in the Eucharist feeds us like a female, out of his own flesh and blood. We are knit into his body, as Lady Julian puts it, where he gives birth to us, each of us, waiting on us like a patient mother until we are all, in each part, caught up into the life of the spirit. The spirit enters our bodies like food – to be chewed, swallowed, drunk; to nourish our feebleness into strength. It is a new life that still includes suffering, loss, even death.

The good does not annihilate the bad but binds it up and brings us through it into something different. What seemed an inevitable result is transmuted into the operation of new creative forces. What seemed lost is refigured as found; what was broken, as mended; what was damned, as forgiven. The good does not banish evil or death, but it does persist. It does not quit any of us, but enters us undefeated, as itself, shining like the pearl or the potent seed. Its insistence on its presence and its appearance in the most unlikely places give weight to those words of Paul that neither principalities nor powers, neither death nor life, can separate us from the love of God.

The creative power of people who correspond to the good has a presence that acts as a linking force to bring all things together. It reconstructs broken parts. It unites other people. It is more than mere passing goodness. It is constructive where everything else is destructive and is so with such persistence and persuasion and over such a long stretch of time that we begin to count upon its presence among us and to depend upon it. We see the power, for example, in the victim of cerebral palsy who faces her handicap with constant good cheer, able to put up with her deformities and to share both her illness and her pleasure with us. We find it in those endlessly useful people whose power is to help others but not to press it upon them, who can be counted on for almost any task but who do not intrude themselves into others' lives in the doggedly demanding way of the do-gooder. We find fulfill-ment simply because that power is with us. We look for it as on a depressingly cloudy day we look for the sun. We reach for its analgesic relief as we never do for a painkiller. It is clearly not a nostrum, a quick fix, a means of forgetting or suppress-ing unpleasantness and suffering. It – or rather, he or she – carries our suffering for us and with us. The suffering servant moves among us and we know peace.

What we experience this way is what we might call original virtue, as opposed to original sin. In people of this kind, there is a residual goodness that seems always to have been there and never to depart. These people are what the words of Scripture and the rhetoric of ancient moral theology, all somewhat remote to the modern mind, are about as they attempt to describe the figure of a saint or *alter Christus* or almost anyone of uncommon virtue. What we must under-stand is that Paul, Augustine, Luther, Calvin are discussing a world of substance, are talking about real behavior and real people, not cardboard figures of goodness. They knew such people; they were such people. They had persevered and found wholeness in their own disjointed lives and those of others. They had dealt with epilepsy, violent stomach disorders, and what they saw as inordinate sexual desire or excessive need for political power and personal preferment. They knew human limitations well and, more important, they knew how to be enlarged by those limitations and to triumph over them. To their listeners and readers, those close to them in physical or historic existence, what they were talking about was entirely recognizable. They were convincing, not because their audiences were more credulous than later generations, but because they spoke with the unmistakable conviction of experience – their own and that of those around them – of a towering goodness, of a deeply planted and all but instinctive virtue. For them, this was reality at least as much as sin, and the essential reason for condemning and moving to extirpate all those human frailties and fallibilities that get in the way of such a productive goodness.

In a secularist age, the language of virtue wears a smirk. The goodness it seeks to make commendable belongs in fairy tales. It is simply not convincing to most people. But still they go on reading fairy tales, or their even less persuasive imitations, Gothic romances, or whatever form of love adventure may at any moment catch their fancy. And they go on dreaming. In both the realm of consciousness and the realm of the unconscious, Cinderella and Prince Charming retain their hallowed roles. The suffering servant and the noble rescuer may walk less openly among us, but they have not disappeared and they will never go very far away. We need what they bring us symbolically. We have to hope this way, to believe that flesh-and-blood human beings can bring a palpable goodness into our world. We demand our Christ figures, large-scale or small-scale, with or without a varnish of romance. We fight this way against all the fragmentation of our lives, the massive destruction and the trivial. We look to some way to hold the pieces together, to effect a marriage of the parts that cannot exist except in devastating disharmony unless united. We look to someone. It may even be ourselves.

Goodness connects all the parts – and all the people – when it is allowed to do so. That is why the familiar image of the realm of God as city or community endures; we understand that what is really good is shared by all inhabitants. Goodness, when we go out to meet it, no longer seems an object possessed by one sector to the exclusion of another. It is shared or it does not exist at all.

When goodness is envisioned as a community, we mean we are in communion with one another, sharing the same food and drink, feeling an interpenetration of our distinct selves, the parts that make up the human whole. Selves neither withdraw into isolated separateness nor fuse together, losing their individual identity. Interdependence replaces infantile dependence on others. We still have needs; they are unavoidable and appropriate parts of our human condition. We carry and experience them, suffer them, if necessary. At our best, we answer them in each other and find them answered in ourselves. Either/or gives way to both/and, as a story of the feast of heaven makes clear. In it, an abundance of food stands before an assembled people. Unhappily, all of the people have a basketlike contraption fastened to both their hands, so that when they try to scoop up the lovely food the basket stops the hand from reaching the mouth. The basket is too long, too big, too clumsy. Heaven is the discovery that each person can partake of the plenty when he feeds his neighbor, for the baskets are perfectly designed to reach from one self to the other, and all can be handsomely fed that way.

Envy is now matched by relief that others do what we cannot or will not; we can rely on their goodness when our own falls short, can depend on their accomplishments when we reach the limits of our own. We are no longer under pressure to do it all ourselves but can share in what others can do. On a small scale, this experience of sharing and interdependence is felt by parents, each of whom counts on the other to provide for their child what one alone cannot do. And when there is only one parent, a matching contribution can be made by an older child, a relative, a close friend. These are the essential links that make life livable.

So it goes with all sharing: the skill of one person supplements that of another. One friend provides a softening another lacks. Coauthors move in and out of a subject according to their skills, reaching into their separate resources as chamber musicians and acrobats do, and knowing them as complete when they are brought together. Human life seems possible then only if shared and carried together. Like a circle of hands and faces, we survive *because* we are linked, each one with each other, some close and touching, some a short distance across the way, some just within viewing distance or communication by letter or phone, but all connected, person to person. We do not bemoan the fact that some have and others have not, but rejoice that as each one has and has not, we can make up for our deficits through the overflowing gifts of others as they can enjoy the flowing over from ourselves to fill in their deficiencies. Mutuality is both an overflow out of abundance and a supplement, even out of a meager supply, to make up for each other's lacks.

We are tutored in mutuality by the example of the arts. When a piece of music works, it works part by part, each fragment fitting into the others with precision, whether it is the endless flow of materials drawn with such economy from a stated theme in a Mozart concerto movement or aria, or, say, the deft crabwise side-mirroring in a Schoenberg twelve-tone composition. When we look at the huge gatherings of details – people and things, textures and colors – in a Brueghel painting, we see every bit fall into place without any one of them losing its individual life. If we move brushstroke by brushstroke into the anatomy of a Cézanne still life, we recognize how each one of the painter's applications achieves an almost independent power while contributing unmistakably to the strength and conviction of all the others and the finished whole.

In a poem, a novel, a play, a film, quality is accomplished by that interdependence of parts which it is the privilege of a knowing reader or spectator to take in and in some way or another hold on to. The goodness that establishes and defines being is a gathering of parts in this way. It brings us presences that depend upon each other, recognizing as we do in appreciation of another's accomplishments that such dependence does not diminish us in any way. On the contrary, we grow with others; we are enlarged by their wit or charm, by their beauty or artful inventiveness, by their imagination, by their goodness.

Goodness displays itself as abundance to those who really see it. Envy sees goodness as a limited supply, like a pie that offers just so many pieces – the bigger the wedge for you, the smaller for me. Envy competes for goodness, whereas goodness shows itself to be more like the manna of Scripture or the tiny seed that grows into a huge tree. Like the loaves and fishes, goodness feeds more than physical hunger, a fact that silences those arguments against goodness which keep demanding to know what use it is to feed a limited number of the poor.

Here again lies the offense of goodness: God's goodness differs altogether from Caesar's. Our versions of the good come smack up against an unscalable goodness. Its height discloses to us our small, partial, feeble view of things.

No wonder we are scandalized and take offense! Another beginning! No wonder we can understand now our savage rejection of the good! It is too much, too other, too different, throwing us out of ourselves to find ourselves beginning at a new point. We can touch here our own participation in what theologians symbolize as original sin.

Even the best of us are tempted here, tempted against goodness. We cannot believe we have hold of anything so substantial, so otherworldly, so much beyond our deserving. This is where so many good people turn superstitious, fancying all sorts of incompetence or failure or simply bad luck that must interfere with the goodness that seems to have come their way. Love is the particular victim in such circumstances. It just seems too good to be true. How can anyone deserve it?

Cinderella's example should tutor us here; we should move forward with every confident expectation to fit ourselves into whatever glass slipper is offered. When we do so, with faith in the real possibilities of goodness and thus of love, we do not exhibit our egoism; we show our trust.

The envied fall very easily into the temptation against goodness. They are so often the objects of extravagant praise by the envying – who do not for a moment see the gifts of others, but only their own failure to possess them – that they have learned to discount any good words thrown their way and even to distrust goodness itself. The envied may or may not realize the envy that stands behind the admiration, but they do sense that it is not trustworthy. As a result, they not only reject the praise of the insincere but begin to doubt almost any offering of the sort – words, friendship, even love. They come to rival the neurotic behavior of the envying in their insecurity with their own gifts. And so the least likely of alliances is made, between the envied and the envying, an alliance in the service of self-doubt and pessimism about human goodness.

The virus of self-doubt and pessimism about others is wildly contagious. We are all sufficiently uncertain about ourselves to be quickly susceptible to anything that may confirm us in our low self-esteem. And we are all just hopeful enough to be proved wrong in this so that anything that can be imputed to others that will raise our low rating of ourselves is bound to be just as catching. The unbeatable combination here is that the pessimism about others does not altogether relieve us of our agony of self-doubt, for all we can know for sure is that others have been undiscriminating in their praise of us. We have no assurance that because they have over-praised us, we deserve any praise at all. We sink further into the extremes of rejection and misunderstanding. We push goodness farther and farther away. It is not for us. We are not for it.

Nonetheless, despite our rejection and incomprehension, goodness continues to offer itself and in abundance – enough to go around and more left over, heaven as an eternal feast. We can participate in the banquet by taking even the tiniest seed of good even in the midst of evil, suffering, and death. We participate in abundance when we choose to taste the good crumb rather than sink into the threatening vacuum of bad thoughts, agonizing failure, illness and loss.

Here, for a moment, husband and wife meet, eyes recognizing and calling out the best in each other, even though one may be dying of cancer and the other of grief.

Here, for a moment, mother and daughter repair the wounded relations of a lifetime, touching hands, seeing and gladly affirming each other, even though one feels near death and the other feels sunk in depressed middle age. In such moments, all that life offers is contained, its depth reaching right to the core of what is important and lasting. For only what is rescued into love will survive.

Here, for a moment, two persons meet as man and woman, touching each other's bodies and reaching into their souls, even if their sexual encounters are drastically uneven or unfulfilled.

Here, for a moment, a stranger riding by in a truck in a winter storm stops to help a man immobilized in a snowdrift in his driveway. Unknown to each other till now, they recognize each other's struggles against skidding and ice – and this way do know each other.

Here, for a moment, a woman travels many hours to be present for her friend at a meeting where that friend will be attacked by others. Her coming will not prevent the attack, but she will not leave her friend to face the attack alone.

Here, for a moment, one sees a beautiful painting that unmistakably displays someone's struggle with pain, despair and death. There, in colors, textures and lines, one person offers hope to another, showing how it was possible to meet those forces and triumph over them, and the viewer goes away filled in the spirit.

Here, for a moment, is a man speaking from his heart to his colleagues at a meeting, without trying to trick or cajole them, just speaking the truth as he sees it. And one of his colleagues, so often fallen away from the truth to the expedient, to the half measure, to the opportune or the equivocating – this colleague feels himself stirred, addressed, called for, and finds himself answering in kind.

Here, for the moment, in the cellar of a house fallen from bombs in a European city during World War II, a mother and her son fight to free themselves from the wreckage that pins them under flooding water that rises to drown them. The mother, being taller, is safe from the water, but hopelessly caught fast under a wooden plank. The child, young and small, is also caught fast on the other side of the cellar, unable to rise above the rushing waters. Just before he drowns, he calls out to his mother to be comforted; it is not so terrible, for she is there with him. What a child! To offer such a crumb of goodness to his mother, crazed with her helplessness to save him!

At the opposite end of human experience cluster those events where we fill up with others in a shared goodness: feeling pulled together by the music in a concert hall; feeling a sense of the transcendent together in a service of worship; dissolving into mirth together. We are positively ejected from seriousness and gloom into a great gale of laughter. We are swept out of ourselves – and into ourselves – by a breathtaking view of a new season: spring, summer, autumn, winter, it does not matter which.

Goodness calls us out of ourselves into glimpsing something beyond ourselves that actually is there among us, the reality we have named the truth, the beautiful, or goodness itself. Goodness also calls us into something well within ourselves – our reality, the truth, the beautiful, the good, the centers of life as only we can understand them. They come to us in the peculiar rhythms, the subtleties of meaning which, however slight may be their differences from the rhythms and understanding peculiar to others, are our own and speak to us and of us as nobody else's can. This is the world of being. This is the world where being comes into its own. There is no place for envy here. We cannot even contemplate the possibility of envy if we have arrived at this place where all our security is in our entrusting ourselves to goodness and its accompanying truth and beauty. Here we must, like Cinderella, be transparent to goodness.

Envy may have been useful to us in coming to this point. We may have learned from the envy of others what it is that we bring with such clarity, conviction and distinction into the world that it prompts the utmost desire in others – desire to the point of envy. We can better understand ourselves and what we possess this way. We can nurture it. We can learn to carry it with such understanding and assurance, with such unmistakable authority, that others may see that it is really ours and fully claimed by us. They may see that to envy us is to deny our right to be who and what we are.

We may have learned from our envy of others what means most to us, what we must have in order to be most fully at ease with our own being. We may or may not be able to accomplish what others have done that we find so alluring. We may lack a talent, a skill, a physical, intellectual, or moral quality that gives the envied other his or her special grace. Our own special grace will be, then, to recognize our own limitations, but not necessarily to relinquish all claim to whatever it is that we envy. We have the possibilities given us by the moral imagination. We can see ourselves in the perspective of our envy and the accomplishments of others. We can nurture, if nothing else, the hope to develop or to become what we want. Failing, for whatever reason, to achieve our end, we can so deepen our appreciation of the accomplishments of others that we become a critic and scholar of the moral purpose or beauty or goodness of others. We do not duplicate others' achievements this way or show our own inadequacy in our attempt to do so; we add something. We enlarge being by confirming and accepting it, both in someone else and in ourselves. It is not a trivial thing to do. We do not simply turn into a groupie, fawning on someone or something. We bring acceptance into our lives, even reverence, as we do when we are brought to awed admiration of a musician's or a dancer's or an actor's performance. This way we nurture quality in the world.

To say this is not to convert envy into a positive factor, a "civilizing" one, as Schoeck does. To make good use of evil does not make it anything other than evil; it simply transforms its effects. We can take some comfort, as Schoeck does, in the fact that envy occasionally results in innovative performance by those determined to "outdo" the envied. But a productive or creative act is not to be attributed to envy. As Schoeck says, in his attempt to view envy in some positive light, "The only activity that liberates from envy is that which fills us with different impulses, feelings and thoughts which, to be of help, have to be value-asserting, dynamic and forward-looking."[99] In other words, envy must be subverted, defeated, replaced. It may, at some distant point, have been the energizing factor for the first spiral of activity that has led, finally, to something fresh and innovative. But the assertion of positive value that Schoeck describes is not in any significant sense an effect of envy. Rooted in being, a movement of positive value is entirely against the destructive forces of envy.

In the name of envy, we claim what belongs to someone else. In the name of being, we claim what belongs to us. We cannot take away somebody else's being and make it our own. We must see it, no matter how admirable and attractive, as utterly foreign to us. It cannot be transplanted in us; the organs of our spirit would reject it with a finality greater than any displayed by the body in refusing a new liver or heart. We may come to give accommodation to a new auricle or ventricle, as some have been able to do; we can never really absorb the person that those chambers once animated. We may be enlarged by others, deepened, made to make better use of the person we are. But we can only be our own person, and every attempt to be another one must be a disaster for us and for all around us.

The effort to cut away and reshape our persons to fit another's form is as much a mockery of human behavior as the surgery with which the ugly sisters hack away at their feet to make them fit Cinderella's glass slipper. The fatuity of such a performance may not be so quickly apparent as in the case of the stepsisters. Its long-lasting effects on society may not come at all to mind as we move more and more into a world where failure and incompetence are not often allowed to be identified and where the inversion of ancient prejudices so frequently obscures individual accomplishments in the name of racial or sexual justice.

The point is that envy has existed and does exist. The answer to it is not legislation that seeks to banish some of its effects by declaring an equality that never has existed and never can, an equality not of opportunity but of achievement. The suffering servant is a more useful figure in this moral and psychological combat than the egalitarian legislator or judge, and a far more realistic one. He or she, Cinderella or *alter Christus,* anyone of this grace-filled persuasion, offers us the opportunity to see ourselves and to accept ourselves with whatever we have or do not have. A false perception does not come this way, but neither does any opprobrium attach itself to us because we have not accomplished what we simply are not equipped to accomplish. We see ourselves instead as we must see ourselves and accept the world as we must accept it. We recognize evils where they exist and the possibilities of goodness. We do not confuse the one for the other or engage in that worst of civil wars which results from the confusion, a war of hatred in which we fight against ourselves or our society for not being what we insist they must be, in spite of all the evidence that they can never be.

Envy, the enemy of being, is central to all of this, and all the more so because it is so rarely admitted to our inspection or contemplation. We suffer from it. We live in its battlefield. Now we must move to soften the suffering and end the war. We can only do so by going beyond the facile rhetoric of dismissal with which envy is quickly condemned and then just as quickly hidden or forgotten so that we do not have to face the disagreeable facts of its existence. If we do, we may be surprised to find that, as with Cinderella, as with all suffering servants, there are blessings that await us, not the least of them the blessings we bring to others.

A Postscript

15

Refusal

In envy, we project our evil as well as our good, our thieving, our destructive intent, our burning focus. Others must carry our mistakes, too, which then leads us to hold them responsible for our failure and nasty behavior.

We refuse to take the life offered and accuse others of stealing it. We end up not projecting the good but instead project our refusal of it. Then we accuse the other of running off with the good, of hoarding it, withholding it, hiding it.

When treatment succeeds, we feel humiliated and will not take the success in order to foil the therapist and to make the therapist feel impotent. We refuse to suffer our own experience or to admit to desire or to need because that wiliness would make us too vulnerable. Then we sabotage the good that may come to us through therapy in order to go on refusing both our own desire and need and the therapist onto whom we have projected the good. We envy our therapists for possessing the good with which we endow them. We envy the therapist's contact with the good in us, with our own unconscious, which we have refused to receive, and proceed to accuse the therapist of ganging up on us in cahoots with our own unconscious.

If we recognize the other as a good object, our own omnipotence is threatened, so we must refuse the other such recognition and deny our dependence on the other. Then we can spiral down into the ritual of destroying the good object (the other) and the good we have put into the other. The part of us that engaged with the other profitably gets kidnapped by the parts of us that refuse in concert with the parts of us that remain unlived. All these parts operate like a gang, mugging the central part in us that connects with the good. Refusing the convenant bond with the other that would allow a creative regression – working our way down to the good we long for, an acknowledged desire and need – turns into a cataclysmic regression. We lose both self and other. The direct implications for crime and social violence are large.

Why are we envied? Many people of merit do not attract envy. Why, then, do the envied attract envy? We will explore two different routes. The first is when the envied one wants to attract envy, usually to substitute for love undelivered and inexperienced. The person who flashes riches, wit, fame, beauty, power over employees or rivals, seeks the envy of others to establish in themselves the self that has been unsupported and unwelcome. Power in the form of seeking to draw on envy replaces love and self-esteem that are grown from the inside. This kind of envied one really enjoys being envied. Envy for such persons is a signature of their existence.

The second route poses a still greater puzzle. Here, the envied suffer others' envy but would be rid of it, if possible. It burns them. They do not want power; they seek love and mutual welcoming. So what is it, then, that attracts others' envy of them? The envied ones, remember, make every effort to avoid envy. Still, envy seeks them out because of their resort to self-holding in the absence of being held – supported – by others, and because their longing for love and their dependence are hidden.

In the book, we have a footnote about a child who seeks to emulate the good. Such persons learn to hold themselves up to make up for lack of parental support and gladness for their being. The child devotes all his or her energy to striving for the good that attracts them to others. Such children seek to build up the good in themselves, to store it up, to fall back on it later in life to meet the dependency that was left unsupported in their early lives. The result is an accomplished person whose deep dependency needs are opaque to the envier but which unmistakably communicate need. This sets up a mysterious connection between the envier, who is feeling without the good, and the envied one, who appears to possess so much of the good – and may indeed do so. The envied one here has a hidden need to depend on others receiving them, affirming them gladly. That need makes this envied one acutely vulnerable to envier's envy. A secret handshake is exchanged. We will explore this serious, important complex problem and its solution.

16

Willingness

We must send out, project, the good or we possess no way to receive its coming to us. In the depths of the mystery of freedom, we are asked to participate in creating the good by wanting it, needing it, choosing it, imagining it. Then we can participate in God's manifesting creativeness.

We need to meditate on the mystery of why we must create the good that we find, or else feel persecuted by it. Winnicott, for example, concludes from his countless observations of the fit between infants and the breasts of their mothers, and in his analyses of adults in a regressed state, that we must project the good outward onto the other in order to receive it ourselves. There, we find the source of the spiritual life which requires for its endurance full contribution from the subject, us, and from the object, the other, God. If either is missing, the good does not fall into place. We envy instead.

Exploring the mystery of creating what we find and finding what we create leads us to recognize the fact that reality consists of multiple interdependencies. We lend our analyst the capacity to do good work in analysis, and the analyst then gives it back to us. Thus, projection does not only defend but also calls goodness to us. It makes the good receivable, or, to put it more accurately, God's graciousness accommodates our smallness by arriving in forms we can accept and receive.

Many illustrations offer themselves – in friendship, teaching, in dreams, in social policy.

17

Envy: Further Thoughts

To begin with, we should like to explain our use of the word "further." These thoughts comprise an addition to extensive earlier work on the phenomenon of envy, looked at in terms of both psychology and religion. We wrote a long study on envy. Indeed, we suffered it, for envy is a dire and costly experience. We told each other, then, that it was like swimming underwater in sludge, fearful we would ever get up to the air again.

We helped ourselves by using the tale of Cinderella, taking as our entry point the experience of being envied. To our great surprise and relief, we discovered good things about envy – not that envy is not all that bad, because it is. Envy is terrible: it vitiates a sense of self; it sabotages relationship to others; it attacks any hope in the good. But we discovered in the course of our study that envy sees the good and salutes the good. If we can get back to the hunger that envy masks, then, we can eat the good, even if just the little crumb of it that belongs to us. Hungry envy, thus helps us break up an abstract, monolithic, idealized good that exceeds our grasp and begins to feed on the little real good before us. When envy is around, so, too, is goodness. This discovery amazed us, and so we set to work to explore the vicissitudes of the relationship of envy and the good. Our conclusions are found in this book.

Our purpose here is to state as simply as possible new thoughts that should be added to those conclusions. The central idea turns around a question prompted by D.W. Winnicott's description of early infant feeding. The question is: Why do we have to create the good we find, or else feel persecuted by it, as Winnicott concludes from his observations of the fit between infant and breast and in his analyses of adults in a regressed state? Why are we not glad there is a good there, external to us, and glad to be dependent on those who hand it to us, instead of feeling envious of their ability to do so, or invaded by their efforts?

Winnicott explains clearly that envy arises in an infant when the infant's projection of the good is met just well enough by a good-enough mother for the infant to feel there is a good there, existing in its own right, ready to meet the infant's need. But this meeting does not happen regularly or reliably, and so the good seems too out of reach to the infant. The link between the baby's projection and the reality of the good is not reliably sustained. The good is tantalizingly both there and not there, and the baby succumbs to envy.

The adult patient, working his or her way back to the experience of rupture from the good, stumbles onto envy on the way. It turns up, for example, as envy of an analyst's ability to do analysis, to offer the good needed. "Why should my analyst have this good instead of me?!" the patient demands, and often will not relinquish the doing of the analysis to the analyst, for fear of a repetition of the tantalizing or persecuting experience.

We can also see why pride stands alongside envy, occupying the highest place in the list of Seven Deadly Sins that dates back to medieval times. Pride means, "I am the Good. I don't need you to give it to me. I am altogether self-sufficient." The undoing of envious pride and phantom self-sufficiency follows up on our acknowledgment of the fact of dependence. Winnicott says, with his usual eloquent brevity: "Gratitude is dependence that is acknowledged." [100]

This returns us to our question: Why do we have to create what we find in order to find it, and why do we have to find it in order to create it? Whether we are talking about the good breast meeting the hungry child, or a teacher matching the right material to a student's idea, or the love of a friend answering our moment of panic, we are in each case pointing to the good in action. At this point of meeting, matching and answering, we find the origin of the spiritual life. For the life of the spirit requires contribution from the subject, the self, and from the object, the other. If either is missing, the good just does not fall into place, and that mysterious space of the spirit that reaches deep inside us and far outside us does not begin or find the impulse to do so.

The answer to the question then is, we think, that we have to create the good and come to know it in some fullness because reality is a network of interdependence. We must imagine and project outward our vision of the good in order to find it fitting our vision. As an infant, we may believe, if Winnicott is right, that we ourselves conjure up the good object. As adults, this imagining and our wish for the good are tantamount to our bringing it into being. It may be what some theologians mean by calling us co-creators with God. We cannot find the good without making it available in this way. The patient lends the analyst the capacity to do good analysis, and the analyst then gives it back.

We must then revise our understanding of the psychological function of projection. Projection is not only a defense maneuver to expel the bad or simply a means of noticing what is there.[101] It also calls goodness to us. This calling may be an adult form of the baby's hunger for the good breast. In it we can acknowledge our dependence on the good. We want it; we need it; we love it.

A student who calls out in this way is easy to teach because he or she uses creatively what the teacher offers. An analysand who calls to us in the same fashion is wonderful to work with because he or she makes such immediate inventive application of what the psyche unfolds. Lovers of this kind are a joy to love and to be loved by because they so gladly form into wondrous bequests everything that is given them. Such believers are loved by God because they are never lukewarm, but rather, eager to find, devise and originate new good things out of what has been given them. We can feel this connection as a sort of humming within our own psyche when a dream actually replies to a question we are asking. All these instances of the right fit arouse in us emotions of wonder, excitement and joy.

The humming interdependence of energy that wants to be in you, in us, in plants, in animals, in politics, moves us to enter its current. We do that by projecting out our pictures of the goods we love, depend upon and want to gobble up.

A second answer to the question arises here: We must send out our projections, our bridges to the good, because the good, in itself, as an external object or energy, is so big compared to our little vision of it that it scares us. It could squash us. It is like a huge snake that takes an unusual interest in us. Our first reaction is to find some way to get away from it, as one woman dreamt. It is like a primordial Spider that contains a treasure, to cite one man's dream, that filled the dreamer, both in the dream and out of it, with dread.

Without our little pictures of God, God overwhelms us. Without our bridges to this energy, it burns us up. Without our tiny ego-imaginings, the Self defeats us. Without this mysterious element of the creative in us – which is ours, which defines us – creativity quells us. We cannot house it or any part of it.

The answer points to the gap between the enormous good and our little good sent out into the world, like a delicate tendril. Where they meet is something like Michelangelo's creation scene on the ceiling of the Sistine chapel. Our spiritual life, our authenticity, is what weaves back and forth across the gap, there where we find our little goods met by the great all, but overwhelming goods, there where we find, lose and are found by the central current of energy that goodness offers us.

God needs us not for consciousness, as Jung says, but for loving, out and back, forth and back, in and out, creating a whole living network of goods projected and received and thrust forward into the world again.

Notes

1. See "A Note on the Psychological Literature on Envy," pp. 177-179.
2. All analytic case examples, unless otherwise noted, come from Ann Ulanov's practice as an analyst, and are used with permission of the people involved, for which we are grateful.
3. Helmut Schoeck, *Envy, A Theory of Social Behavior* trans. Michael Glenny and Betty Ross (Harcourt, Brace and World, 1966), p. 179; see also pp. 167, 195, 210, 258.
4. Max Scheler says that the worst form of envy is the "existential" which is "forever muttering 'I could forgive you anything, except *that* you are, and *what* you are; except that I am not what you are; that "I," in fact, am not "you."' This 'envy,' from the start, most strongly denies the other person his very existence." (Schoeck, *Envy*, p. 183).
5. The temptation of the envied one to make himself into a self-sufficient ideal object can be confused with another response to envy that appears to be the same but springs from quite different motives. This response to being envied is to emulate the good.
For example, a child who is a victim of a parent's envy cannot get the good things needed from that parent, like love, security, and guidance, because the parent's envy keeps interfering. The child is left with a gap between itself and the good. One possible response is emulation: the child then goes after the good with singular dedication and determination, in order to close the gap, trying to make the most of whatever skill it has or can learn from others, working hard to be good at sports studies, hobbies, friendship, whatever makes up a child's world. Often quite remarkable accomplishments result.
The emulating child's zealous dedication to getting close to the good seems like the compulsion of a child who aims to *become* the ideal all-perfect good. Both children often achieve a lot and may become targets of others' envy, but the motives of the two children differ sharply. The emulator strives toward the good out of longing for it, hoping to draw closer to it; the other child, in its victimized state, wants to replace the good out of fear of the bad – to escape the stinging attacks of enviers. The emulator's efforts spring out of relation to the good; the other wants to substitute itself for the good.
Both children are more independent than average. Both have the

task of learning how to risk depending on others. The emulator will find this task easier, because of a real hunger for the good that will always attract other people, whom the child can take in and identify with, thus peopling its intrapsychic world at the same time as it builds intimacy with others. The sad fate awaiting the one who would become an ideal, totally self-sufficient good-in-itself, in order to escape envy, is to discover that that route evokes even more envy.

6. Schoeck points out that social revolutions in developing countries often go after the citizen who has become an object of envy because of any advantage, no matter how small, over others, often interpreted by the envious as unjust and deliberately so. Schoeck gives the examples of persons murdered because they owned a sewing machine or had studied for a semester in a foreign school. See Schoeck, *Envy*, p. 346, and also pp. 225, 275, 280.

7. Simone Weil, *Waiting for God*, trans. Emma Craufurd (G. P. Putnam's Sons, 1951), p. 112.

8. Melanie Klein, *Envy and Gratitude, and Other Works, 1946-1963* (Delacorte Press, 1975), p. 205.

9. Hanna Segal, *Introduction to the Work of Melanie Klein* (London: William Heinemann, 1964), pp. 27-29, and Hanna Segal, *Melanie Klein* (Viking Press, 1979), p. 146.

10. See Edmund Spenser, *The Faerie Queene*, Book I, iv. 30; the pageant of the Seven Deadly Sins in Christopher Marlowe's *Doctor Faustus;* and John Bunyan, *The Pilgrim's Progress*, Trial of Christian and Faithful.

11. Erich Neumann, *The Origins and History of Consciousness*, trans. R. F. C. Hull (Pantheon Books, 1954), p. 46.

12. Harold F. Searles, *Collected Papers on Schizophrenia and Related Subjects* (International Universities Press, 1965), pp. 221-223.

13. D. W. Winnicott, *Playing and Reality* (London: Tavistock Publications, 1971), pp. 111-112.

14. C. G. Jung, *Two Essays on Analytical Psychology*, 2d ed., ed. Gerhard Adler et al., trans. R. F. C. Hull, in *The Collected Works of C. G. Jung*, Vol. 7 (Pantheon Books, 1966), pp. 139ff.

15. "Envy attacks the good object and, by projection and fragmentation, makes it bad; therefore it produces a state of confusion between good and bad, which is at the root of many psychotic confusions." (Segal, *Melanie Klein*, p. 147).

16. Harry Guntrip, *Schizoid Phenomena, Object-Relations and the Self* (International Universities Press, 1969), p. 260. We are indebted to Judith Hubback's illuminating distinction between two types of envy, "the genetically earlier, hungry wanting form and the

later or shadow form." See "Envy and the Shadow," *Journal of Analytical Psychology,* Vol. 17, No. 2 (1972), p. 152.

17. Otto Kernberg discusses this as a patient acting out his feelings toward the analyst rather than reflecting upon them. See Otto F. Kernberg, *Borderline Conditions and Pathological Narcissism* (Jason Aronson, 1975), p. 85.

18. Klein, *Envy and Gratitude,* pp. 185, 216-220. See also Nathan Schwartz-Salant, *Narcissism and Character Transformation: The Psychology of Narcissistic Character Disorders* (Toronto: Inner City Books, 1982), pp. 24, 42.

19. Segal, *Melanie Klein,* pp. 149-151.

20. For a discussion of this process of differentiation, see Michael Fordham, "Individuation and Ego Development," *Journal of Analytical Psychology,* Vol. 3, No. 2 (1958), pp. 115-130.

21. Segal, *Melanie Klein,* pp. 150-151.

22. Ibid., pp. 152-153.

23. For an interesting discussion of the hearth symbolism see Bruno Bettelheim, *The Uses of Enchantment* (Alfred A. Knopf, 1976), pp. 254-255.

24. Erich Neumann, *Depth Psychology and a New Ethic,* trans. Eugene Rolfe (G. P. Putnam's Sons, 1969), p. 54.

25. Marie Louise von Franz, *Problems of the Feminine in Fairy Tales* (Spring Publications, 1972), pp. 161-162.

26. The reference is to the title character in Bertolt Brecht's play, *The Resistible Rise of Arturo Ui* (1941).

27. Klein, *Envy and Gratitude,* p. 176, and Kernberg, *Borderline Conditions,* pp. 228, 231-235, 241. As for Jung, he does not investigate envy in detail, but his conviction that a child comes into the world equipped with its own psychic stuff is relevant here. That equipment may be negative or positive. It gets into conscious life through the particular "constellating" factors of outer conditions – parents' personalities and their treatment of their child – and inner factors – archetypal images and ideas that assault the ego from the unconscious.

28. See Heinz Kohut, *The Analysis of the Self* (International Universities Press, 1971), pp. 16-17, 27-28, 306; D. W. Winnicott, *The Maturational Processes and the Facilitating Environment* (International Universities Press, 1965), pp. 177-178; and Leslie H. Farber, *Lying, Despair, Jealousy, Envy, Sex, Suicide, Drugs, and the Good Life* (Basic Books, 1976), p. 45.

29. Ann Belford Ulanov, "Fatness and the Female," *Psychological Perspectives,* Vol. 10, No. 1 (1979), pp. 18-36.

30. Farber, *Lying, Despair, Jealousy, Envy,* p. 43.

31. Harold F. Searles, *Countertransference and Related Subjects* (International Universities Press, 1979), p. 233.

32. V. Bukovsky and S. Gluzman, *A Manual on Psychiatry for Dissidents*, a pamphlet published by the Committee Against the Political Misuse of Psychiatry, 5112 Allan Rd., Washington, D.C., 20016.

33. Schoeck, *Envy*, pp. 215, 251; see also pp. 185, 197, 200, 229, 272.

34. See, for example, Hugh of St. Victor as cited by Morton W. Bloomfield, *The Seven Deadly Sins* (Michigan State University Press, 1952), p. 368, n. 163.

35. For a discussion of a masculinized adaptation used as a defense against femaleness, see Karen Homey, "The Flight from Womanhood," in *Feminine Psychology* (W. W. Norton & Co., 1967), pp. 67, 69.

36. Covent Garden Royal Ballet production of Prokofiev's *Cinderella*, broadcast Channel 13, New York City, June 6,1982.

37. Klein, *Envy and Gratitude*, pp. 197, 254; see also Melanie Klein, *The Psycho-Analysis of Children*, trans. Alix Strachey (Delacorte Press, 1975), p. 131.

38. See Irvine Schiffer, *The Trauma of Time* (International Universities Press, 1978), pp. 205, 226-227, for an interesting discussion of oral-genital confusion that can result from envy of the mother.

39. L. P. Hartley, *Facial Justice* (Doubleday & Co., 1961), pp. 45, 208, and *passim*.

40. See below, pp. 109-111.

41. Klein discusses the importance of this differentiation of the parents for the child's development. See Klein, *The Psycho-Analysis of Children*, pp. 132, 246, 253-254.

42. See Bruno Bettelheim, *Symbolic Wounds* (Free Press, 1954), pp. 17, 19, 20, 34; and Wolfgang Lederer, *The Fear of Women* (Grune & Stratton, 1968), pp. 153-154.

43. For a discussion of fear and hatred of the female as representative of being, see Ann Belford Ulanov, *Receiving Woman: Studies in the Psychology and Theology of the Feminine* (Westminster Press, 1981), pp. 80-89.

44. Mary Williams, "Success and Failure in Analysis: Primary Envy and the Fate of the Good," *Journal of Analytical Psychology*, Vol. 17, No. 1 (1972), pp. 7-17; see also Michael Rosenthall, "Notes on Envy and the Contrasexual Archetype," *Journal of Analytical Psychology*, Vol. 8, No. 1 (1963), pp. 65.

45. For a discussion of a woman's stirring in a man his ability to rescue her, see Ann and Barry Ulanov, "Bewitchment," *Quadrant*, Vol. 11, No. 2 (1978), pp. 55, 60.

46. For a discussion of the therapist's taking all the good and leaving all the bad to the patient, see Searles, *Countertransference*, pp. 79-80.

47. For a discussion of the "de-integration" process of ego and self, see Michael Fordham, *Children as Individuals* (G. P. Putnam's Sons, 1970), pp. 113-115. For a discussion of envy which, when it is consciously experienced and accepted, acts as a catalyst for the breakup of an ego-self fusion, see Schwartz-Salant, *Narcissism and Character Transformation*, pp. 42-43.

48. Hubback, "Envy and the Shadow," p. 154.

49. Williams, "Success and Failure in Analysis," p. 15.

50. Searles, *Countertransference*, pp. 490, 496.

51. For a discussion of the transference of the anima to the analyst, see Ann Belford Ulanov, "Transference/Countertransference: A Jungian Perspective," in *Jungian Analysis*, ed. M. Stein (Open Court Publishing Co., 1982), pp. 68-85.

52. See Kernberg, *Borderline Conditions*, pp. 306ff., 235.

53. Bloomfield, *The Seven Deadly Sins*, p. 43.

54. See Book II of the *Ethics* of Aristotle. Alasdair MacIntyre's discussion of Aristotle's treatment of envy is helpful here; see his *A Short History of Ethics* (Macmillan Co., 1966), pp. 65ff.

55. Baruch Spinoza, *Ethics*, III. xxiv, in the T. S. Gregory translation (London: J. M. Dent & Sons, 1955 [1910]), p. 101 and Thomas Hobbes, *Leviathan*, I. 6 (London: J. M. Dent & Sons, 1947 [1914]), p. 28.

56. David Hume, *A Treatise of Human Nature*, II. ii. 8 (London: J. M. Dent & Sons, 1962 [1911]), Vol. 2, pp. 93ff.

57. René Descartes, *The Passions of the Soul*, III. clxxxii-clxxxiv, in *The Philosophical Works of Descartes*, trans. E. S. Haldane and G. R. T. Ross (Cambridge University Press, 1969 [1911, 1931]), pp. 414-415.

58. *A New Catechism*, IV, under "Reverence for Life"; trans. Kevin Smyth (Herder & Herder, 1967), p. 422.

59. Thomas Aquinas, *Summa Theologica*, II. IIae. ii. 10c.

60. *The Arabian Nights' Entertainments*, trans. E. W. Lane (London: Bell, 1925 [1914]), Vol. 1, pp. 81-83.

61. The interpretation of evil as the privation of being – which is to say, of ontological goodness – is usually associated with Augustine, but it has a long history and a full development that takes it beyond association with any one ascription, though it must be said that those in the Augustinian tradition hold to it with particular strength, distinction and clarity.

62. *Notes from the Underground* in *The Short Novels of Dostoevsky* (Dial Press, 1945), pp. 132, 134, 136-137, 217, and *passim*.

63. The book ends in mid-sentence, with words that, whatever their intention, resound with irony: "I call upon you for a closer scrutiny of your duty and obligations, whatever your work upon

this earth may be, for by now our duty is but dimly perceptible to us, and we can hardly...." Nikolai Gogol, *Dead Souls*, trans. as *Chichikov's Journeys* by B. G. Guerney (Heritage Press, 1944), p. 484.

64. Yury Olesha, *Envy*, trans. Thomas S. Berczynski (Ardis Publications, 1975), pp. 76-77, 68, 113-115, and *passim*.

65. Envy infuses the characters of Bazarov in *Fathers and Sons* and Nezhdanov in *Virgin Soil*, by Turgenev. In Tolstoy, comprehension of envy is central to understanding Pierre Bezukhov and Andrei Bolkonsky in *War and Peace* and Karenin and Vronsky in *Anna Karenina*. In Dostoevsky, envy pervades all the conspirators and those conspired against in *The Devils*, Myshkin, Rogozhin, Aglaya, and Nastasia in *The Idiot*, Raskolnikov in *Crime and Punishment*. And this is just to touch major figures, obvious cases.

66. *Mozart and Salieri*, trans. A. F. B. Clark, in *The Works of Alexander Pushkin*, ed. Avrahm Yarmolinsky (Random House, 1936), pp. 428-437.

67. Dante, *Inferno*, Canto VII, line 123.

68. "Hispanic Envy," in Miguel de Unamuno, *Perplexities and Paradoxes*, trans. Stuart Gross (Greenwood Press, 1968 [1945]), pp. 44, 47-48; and Julian Marias Aguilera, *Miguel de Unamuno*, trans. Frances M. López-Mórillas (Harvard University Press, 1966), pp. 44-45, 56, 94-101.

69. Dante, *Purgatorio*, XVII, lines 13-18.

70. Louis Lavelle, *The Dilemma of Narcissus*, trans. William T. Gairdner (London: George Allen & Unwin, 1973), pp. 186-187.

71. Søren Kierkegaard, *The Concept of Dread*, trans. Walter Lowrie (Princeton University Press, 1957), pp. 110, 116, 118.

72. Dante, *Purgatorio*, XIII, lines 70-72, 83-84.

73. Søren Kierkegaard, *The Sickness Unto Death*, trans. Walter Lowrie (Doubleday & Co., Doubleday Anchor Books, 1954 [1941]), pp. 216-217.

74. Søren Kierkegaard, *Fear and Trembling*, trans. Walter Lowrie (Doubleday & Co., Doubleday Anchor Books, 1954 [1941]), pp. 58, 52, 55, 60.

75. Lev Shestov, *Kierkegaard and the Existential Philosophy*, trans. Elinor Hewitt (Ohio University Press, 1969), p. 83.

76. Blaise Pascal, *Pensées*, ed. Louis Lafuma, trans. John Warrington (London: J. M. Dent & Sons, 1961), 246 [536-434], p. 65.

77. Kierkegaard, *The Sickness Unto Death*, p. 215.

78. Ibid., p. 258.

79. Otto Kernberg sees this maneuver as a primary defense against envy, but one that keeps us empty of good objects (*Borderline Conditions*, p. 235).

80. Georg Groddeck, *The World of Man*, trans. V. M. E. Collins (Funk & Wagnalls Co., 1951), pp. 83-86.

81 Kierkegaard, *The Sickness Unto Death*, p. 262.

82. Pascal, *Pensées*, 11 [898-194], p. 8.

83. R. G. Collingwood, *The New Leviathan* (Thomas Y. Crowell Co., 1971 [1942]), 8.31-32, p. 56.

84. Gabriel Marcel, *Tragic Wisdom and Beyond*, trans. Stephen Jolin and Peter McCormick (Northwestern University Press, 1973), p. 146.

85. Elisabeth Langgässer, *The Quest*, trans. Jane B. Greene (Alfred A. Knopf, 1953), pp. 147, 151.

86. Max Scheler, *Ressentiment*, ed. Lewis A. Coser, trans. William W. Holdheim (Free Press of Glencoe, 1961), pp. 77, 81, 126, 124, and *passim*.

87. Schoeck, *Envy*, pp. 61, 132, 299.

88. Ibid., pp. 264, 269, 275.

89. Ibid., pp. 133, 280, 348.

90. José Ortega y Gasset, *Man and People*, trans. Willard R. Trask (W. W. Norton & Co., 1957), pp. 103, 112-138.

91. Scheler, *Ressentiment*, p. 169.

92. Georg Simmel, "The Nobility," trans. R. P. Albares, in *Georg Simmel on Individuality and Social Forms: Selected Writings*, ed. Donald N. Levine (University of Chicago Press, 1971), pp. 200, 206-209, 212-213.

93. S. L. Frank, *God with Us*, trans. Natalie Duddington (Yale University Press, 1946), p. 124.

94. Ibid., p. 80.

95. Augustine, *Homilies on the Gospel According to St. John*, trans. J. G. Sheppard (Oxford: Parker, 1848), Hom. XXXII, on John 7:37-9, Vol. I, p. 469 (translation revised).

96. See Rosemary Gordon, "Narcissism and the Self," *Journal of Analytical Psychology*, Vol. 25, No. 3 (1980), pp. 247-265.

97. For a lengthy discussion of the feminine modality of being, see Ann Belford Ulanov, *The Feminine in Jungian Psychology and in Christian Theology* (Northwestern University Press, 1971), Ch. 9.

98. Vasily Rozanov, *The Apocalypse of Our Time*, trans. Robert Payne and Nikita Romanoff (Praeger Publications, 1977), p. 241.

99. Schoeck, *Envy*, p. 351.

100. Winnicott, D.W. (1962) "The Beginning of a Formulation of an Appreciation and Criticism of Klein's Envy Statement" in

Psychoanalytic Explorations, eds. Clare Winnicott, Ray Shepherd, Madeleine Davis (London: Karnac, 1989).

101. Ulanov, A. (1981) *Receiving Woman: Studies in the Psychology and Theology of the Feminine* (Louisville: Westminster Press).

Glossary

Anima. The feminine part of a man's psyche. Jung calls the anima the archetype of life. It functions to connect a man's ego to contrasexual contents in the unconscious. The anima shows itself in personified forms, reflecting the several levels of conditioning of the anima image. For example, the influence of significant women in a man's life – mother, sister, aunt, etc. – will be evident as will the prevalent images of the feminine in his culture and time, and the primordial images of the feminine that arise in his psyche in response to specific conscious situations, both personal and collective. A man who takes on the task of differentiating his anima will discover dominant images of women residing in himself, both the positive that immediately attract him and the negative that repel him. These images personify the so-called *eros principle* of relatedness and will influence his actual relations with women, as well as his connection to all things feminine.

Animus. The unconscious masculine part of a woman's psyche which shows itself in personified form in images of men – or masculine elements – in dream and fantasy. It personifies what Jung calls the *logos principle* in a woman's psychology, that spirit of truth by which she tries to live. Animus images reflect different levels of influence, extending from the significant males in a woman's personal history – father, brother, etc. – to the dominant cultural images of the masculine in her historical and social context, and to more abiding elemental images of the masculine, such as the wind or sun, penetrating light, or masculine deities in mythology and religion.

The task facing a woman is to become conscious of the animus images that operate in her, influencing her attitudes and notions of truth as well as her relation to men. The animus needs to become differentiated before it can perform its psychic function of connecting her ego to contrasexual contents in the unconscious.

Archetypes. Patterns of readiness of response to age-old elemental human events. They are not really knowable in themselves because they are not fixed in content, but exist only in the form of responses to people and events. What we know of them comes to us through the primordial images to which they give rise, as well as through ideas and the emotional and behavioral patterns that they influence. These images, ideas, behavior patterns and emotions are what become conscious in us. They are filled out by the material of a specific historical time, a social context, and a personal biography. Jung formulated the concept of archetype from repeated observation of recurrent motifs in fairy tales, literature, religion and mythology. These same motifs turn up in countless dreams, fantasies, images, and associations of individuals. In "Cinderella," we find many archetypal motifs, as our treatment suggests.

Ego. The central complex of consciousness, what we ordinarily associate as "me," the center of conscious identity. Jung understands an individuated person to be one who knows that the ego is only the center of the conscious part of the psyche, and that it needs to relate to the *self,* which is the center of the whole psyche, conscious and unconscious. Paying attention to the self comprises the ego's contribution to maintaining and developing the *ego-self axis,* which is experienced by the ego as an attempt to relate to the center of the personality which transcends its own ego perspectives and purposes. Jung believes the ego's relation to this transpersonal center may be depicted in religious imagery.

Introjection. A process that complements projection. Here we take into ourselves parts of the world and others. They inhabit us, not as mental concepts, or dead pieces of information, or remote memories no longer quite alive, but as lively centers of being to which we constantly react. The terms "introjects," "introjected objects," or "internal objects" refer to this inner population whose origin lies outside ourselves. Jung, in distinction from other depth psychologists, emphasizes that our psychic world comprises, in addition to these objects or parts of objects from the outside world, others that arise spontaneously from the *objective psyche*, that unconscious layer of the psyche which exists antecedent to ego consciousness and gives rise to it. This part of our inner-objects world consists of archetypal images that greatly influence what we take in from outer persons as much as outer persons help shape the way we experience archetypes. The personality of our actual mother, for example, influences the living image of a mother we carry within and what we select from the wide range of possibilities of the mother archetype to concretize in our psychology. The particular archetypal readiness to form a mother image very much influences the way we experience our own mother's personality. This helps account for the ever-puzzling fact that different children with the same parents and home conditions will react in very different ways. The notion of archetype helps conceptualize the unknown factors that children bring into the world and thus is a way of understanding how they seek or create the experiences that define their psychologies.

Part-Object. A term coined by Melanie Klein and used by many other depth psychologists to denote a part of an object or person instead of the whole. Developmentally, we first apprehend part of the whole before we achieve the capacity to perceive whole persons in their autonomous entirety. An important facet of part-object-relating is that the relationship is one-way only: the part refers exclusively to oneself – how one feels about the part-object, uses it, rejects it, or takes it in – with little or no reference to the whole to which the part belongs. In part-object-relating, one's self occupies center stage, as if the parts of others existed only for one's own use. The object as a whole, existing in its own right, does not yet come into consciousness. Only at later stages of development do we achieve capacity for whole-object-relating, which is to say for mutuality.

Projection. A process by which we throw out onto other people our own emotional reactions, perceiving them as originating in someone else. Our subjective emotions now live out there in the objective world as attributes of other people. Projection operates as a basic defense against pain and turmoil, for with it we dispel a troublesome conflict or ugly attitude by ejecting it from ourselves onto others, whom we then blame for the difficulty. We may even altogether identify projectees with this content we have put onto them, now defining them in its terms, a mechanism called *projective identification*. Jung, in particular, emphasizes that projection is not just a defense mechanism but also a normal route by which we become conscious of contents with which we may have been in unconscious identity. We first see such a content in our neighbor's face and react to it, usually with an agitation which betrays that the content in some way belongs to us. Then we face the hard task of sorting out how it does, always an uncomfortable process because, whether the content is positive or negative, our ego has chosen to ignore or disown it. To claim the content now requires a radical change in our self-image and world view.

Shadow. Those contents found unacceptable to ego standards and consequently repressed into unconsciousness, or simply ignored. The ego tries to defend against these contents, expel them or disown them. But they, too, belong to the whole personality, and the ego must come to recognize, claim and integrate them if it would move toward wholeness. Shadow contents are personified in dreams in persons of the same sex, and may turn out to be valued gifts of new energy and points of view to the ego if recognized and assimilated.

A Note on the Psychological Literature on Envy

Melanie Klein is noted for her view that envy is innate, arising spontaneously in an infant from birth as she sees it, in tandem with love and gratitude, in response to the maternal breast. She takes envy as evidence for the existence of a death-instinct in human beings, yet finds it an essential aspect of human psychology that can give rise to efforts at restitution and creativity as well. See Melanie Klein, *Envy and Gratitude, and Other Works, 1946-1963* (Delacorte Press, 1975).

Harold Searles finds envy unavoidable in countertransference reactions to patients in treatment. The therapist must suffer his or her envy consciously. Otherwise, the patient must face the therapist's unconscious provocation, stealing the center of attention, playing the all-good, dedicated physician, leaving the patient to carry all that is bad in the relationship. See Harold F. Searles, *Countertransference and Related Subjects* (International Universities Press, 1979), pp. 274-275, 592.

Harry Stack Sullivan classifies envy as one of the substitutive activities we engage in to ward off an intolerable anxiety. See Harry Stack Sullivan, *Conceptions of Modern Psychiatry* (W. W. Norton & Co., 1953), and his *The Interpersonal Theory of Psychiatry*, ed. Helen Swick Perry and Mary Ladd Gawel (W. W. Norton & Co., 1953), pp. 255, 347-348, 355.

For **Otto Kernberg**, envy is a central and inevitable affliction besetting persons suffering from narcissistic character disorders, because both their internal and external object-relations are pathologically twisted. One feels lifeless inside because unconsciously assailed by crushing self-judgments, aroused by one's own envious attacks on anyone who would be forthcoming to oneself. Thus, one takes nothing in and feels empty. Relations with others yield constant envy, even hatred, over the possibility that they may get and keep, more than oneself. Thus, one always feels alone and unloved. See Otto F. Kernberg, *Borderline Conditions and Pathological Narcissism* (Jason Aronson, 1975), pp. 227-237, 335-337.

Heinz Kohut disagrees with Kernberg about the origin of envy in persons suffering from narcissistic disorder. Rather than a symptom of a pathological core, envy arises from neglect. Envious persons failed to get adequate empathetic relating from their parents. The result is an envious style of perceiving self and others. See Heinz Kohut, *The Analysis of the Self* (International Universities Press, 1971), pp. 181n, 195.

Michael Rosenthall studied envy in relation to the emergence of the contrasexual archetype, the anima in men and the animus in women. Massive envy, he finds, ties a person to his or her mother and prevents the differentiation of the contrasexual side of the personality. See Michael Rosenthall, "Notes on Envy and the Contrasexual Archetype," *Journal of Analytical Psychology*, Vol. 8, No. 1 (1963), pp. 65-75.

Mary Williams investigates the relation of envy to an inability to take in whatever goodness is offered. See Mary Williams, "Success and Failure in Analysis: Primary Envy and the Fate of the Good," *Journal of Analytical Psychology*, Vol. 17, No. 1 (1972), pp. 7-17.

Judith Hubback distinguishes early levels of envy from later ones, where shadow components of hating enter. See Judith Hubback,

"Envy and the Shadow," *Journal of Analytical Psychology,* Vol. 17, No. 2 (1972), pp. 152-166.

Nathan Schwartz-Salant discusses envy in the narcissistic character disorder from a Jungian point of view, finding it not only an affliction but also a catalyst for transformation. If persons suffering from narcissistic character disorder can suffer their envy consciously, its wounding can make them look beyond themselves to the reality of other people and inward to the reality of their needs and feelings. These experiences serve to hasten the breakup of their defensively maintained, grandiose self, directing them toward their own path of individuation. See Nathan Schwartz-Salant, *Narcissism and Character Transformation: The Psychology of Narcissistic Character Disorders* (Toronto: Inner City Books, 1982), pp. 26, 42-43.

Helmut Schoeck, in his sociological study of envy, develops a theory that enlarges on psychological understanding of the subject. Envy is a social phenomenon necessary to group formation and coherence, yet also a barrier that must be broken if a society is to achieve technological and cultural progress. Fear of others' envy and of one's own envious attacks on others checks rampant individualism and thus stabilizes group life. But too much fear of envy can block innovation, invention, and the development of original ideas that will advance the life of society. See Helmut Schoeck, *Envy, A Theory of Social Behavior,* trans. Michael Glenny and Betty Ross (Harcourt, Brace and World, 1966), pp. 2, 3, 10, 11, 57, 58, 197, 348, 350.

Index

Other Daimon Books by Ann & Barry Belford Ulanov:

The Healing Imagination

The Meeting of Psyche and Soul

This eloquent work speaks of the centrality of imagination in the life of the spirit. Ann and Barry Ulanov describe the imagination as a bridge between the psyche and the spirit. Using rich imagery drawn from literature, film, and their own experience as therapists, they unlock for us the healing power of our imagination. "Imagination heals by building a bridge sturdy enough to link us up, each of us, to the river of being already present in us, to the currents flowing through us and among us in our unconscious life." After describing this healing power of imagination, the authors go on to show how it is vital in the spiritual life: in preaching, prayer, teaching, counseling, and politics. (192 pages, ISBN 3-85630-591-2)

The Wizards' Gate

This book, adapted from the distinguished Hale Lectures presents material from a woman's wrestling with death, showing how inextricably mixed are matters theological and psychological.

At a point when her life was blossoming in every way, Nancy was struck down by a terminal brain tumor which soon robbed her of her speech. She used paintings, many of which are here reproduced, to wrestle with this blow and to communicate what she was slowly discerning in the face of death, something from the 'other side.'

The author addresses a variety of related issues, including the place of language in analysis and the role of the feminine mode of being, especially in transference and countertransference. (135 p., color illustrations, ISBN 3-85630-539-4)

The Female Ancestors of Christ

Tamar, Rahab, Ruth, and Bathsheba are the only women mentioned by name in the Gospels' genealogies, showing that they impart something essential to the lineage of Christ. By exploring their unconventional lives, the author demonstrates how salvation enters the world through their embodiment of such powerful and deeply feminine qualities as ingenuity, audacity, determination, compassion, seduction, and devotion. (144 pages, ISBN 3-85630-579-3)

Available from your bookstore or from our distributors:

In the United States:		*In Great Britain:*
Continuum	Chiron Publications	Airlift Book Company
P.O. Box 7017	400 Linden Avenue	8 The Arena
La Vergne, TN 37086	Wilmette, IL 60091	Enfield, Middlesex EN3 7NJ
Phone: 800-937 5557	Phone: 800-397 8109	Phone: (0181) 804 0400
Fax: 615-793 3915	Fax: 847-256 2202	Fax: (0181) 804 0044

Worldwide:

Daimon Verlag   Hauptstrasse 85   CH-8840 Einsiedeln   Switzerland
Phone: (41)(55) 412 2266   Fax: (41)(55) 412 2231
e-mail: info@daimon.ch   www.daimon.ch
Write for our complete catalog!

ENGLISH PUBLICATIONS BY **DAIMON**

Abt / Bosch / MacKrell *Dream Child – Creation and New Life in Dreams of Pregnant Women*

Susan R. Bach
- *Life Paints its Own Span*
- *Images, Meanings and Connections (ed. by Ralph Goldstein)*

E.A. Bennet
- *Meetings with Jung*

George Czuczka
- *Imprints of the Future*

Heinrich Karl Fierz
- *Jungian Psychiatry*

von Franz / Frey-Rohn / Jaffé
- *What is Death?*

Liliane Frey-Rohn
- *Friedrich Nietzsche*

Yael Haft
- *Hands: Archetypal Chirology*

Siegmund Hurwitz
- *Lilith, the First Eve*

Aniela Jaffé *From the Life und Work of C.G. Jung*
- *The Myth of Meaning*
- *Was C.G. Jung a Mystic?*
- *Death Dreams and Ghosts*

Verena Kast
- *A Time to Mourn*
- *Sisyphus*

Hayao Kawai *Dreams, Myths and Fairy Tales in Japan*

James Kirsch
- *The Reluctant Prophet*

Yehezkel Kluger & Nomi Kluger-Nash *A Psychological Interpretation of Ruth*

Mary Lynn Kittelson
- *Sounding the Soul*

Rivkah Schärf Kluger
- *The Gilgamesh Epic*

Paul Kugler *Jungian Perspectives on Clinical Supervision*

Eva Langley-Dános
- *Prison on Wheels: From Ravensbrück to Burgau*

Rafael López-Pedraza
- *Hermes and His Children*
- *Cultural Anxiety*

Gitta Mallasz (Transcription)
- *Talking with Angels*

Alan McGlashan *The Savage and Beautiful Country*
- *Gravity and Levity*

C.A. Meier
- *Healing Dream and Ritual*
- *A Testament to the Wilderness*
- *Personality*

Laurens van der Post
- *The Rock Rabbit and the Rainbow*

Rainer-Maria Rilke
- *Duino Elegies*

Miguel Serrano
- *C.G. Jung and Hermann Hesse: A Record of Two Friendships*

Helene Shulman
- *Living at the Edge of Chaos*

Susan Tiberghien
- *Looking for Gold*

Ann Ulanov
- *The Wizards' Gate*
- *The Female Ancestors of Christ*

Ann & Barry Ulanov
- *Cinderella and Her Sisters*
- *The Healing Imagination*

Erlo van Waveren
- *Pilgrimage to the Rebirth*

Jungian Congress Papers:

Jerusalem 1983 *Symbolic and Clinical Approaches*

Berlin 1986 *Archetype of Shadow in a Split World*

Paris 1989
- *Dynamics in Relationship*

Chicago 1992
- *The Transcendent Function*

Zürich 1995 *Open Questions in Analytical Psychology*

Florence 1998
- *Destruction and Creation*